HOW TO READ

Faces

HOW TO READ
Faces

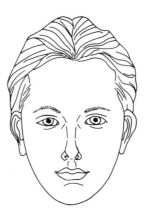

HAMLYN

First published in 1989 by The Hamlyn Publishing Group Limited,
a division of the Octopus Publishing Group
Michelin House
81 Fulham Road
London SW3 6RB

Text and illustrations taken from the work
Conoscerti, Enciclopedia dei Test
© 1986 Gruppo Editoriale Fabbri SpA
Milan

ISBN 0-600-56451-7

Produced by Mandarin Offset
Printed and bound in Hong Kong

Contents

Introduction

Faces will always fascinate people, and reactions to them are many and varied. We fall in love with them, are frightened by them, repelled, bored, impressed or dismissive of them, but rarely are we totally indifferent to them.

Physiognomy, or the art of character reading from the face and body, is an ancient pursuit. In China, where it is known as *Siang Mien*, it is also used to delve into someone's past and predict their future. In the West, it is sometimes combined with phrenology, which claims to give insight into the mind through the study of the indentations on the head.

The Ancient Greeks believed in the authenticity of physiognomy, likening the human face to various types of animal and bird. Such resemblances were said to give reliable character indications – an equine person looked like a horse, and was sincere, affable and generous. The unfortunate possessor of an asinine, or ass-like, face was, like the animal, stubborn, lazy and coarse.

By the nineteenth century, Western physiognomy had become much more sophisticated. Johann Kaspar Lavater, a Swiss clergyman, poet, and mystic, devoted much of his spare time to studying faces, and published a lavishly illustrated book on the subject – with a chapter by his friend Goethe.

Shakespeare, too, was one of the many gifted people who searched for links between character and appearance. Indeed, elaborate masks, wigs and make-up have always been used in the theatre to enhance characterization. During the silent film era stars like Charlie Chaplin (pictured left) deliberately exaggerated their features and gestures. Their audiences were certain to read facial messages loud and clear. Whether consciously or not, experts and amateurs alike form lasting opinions when they first look at a face.

Throughout the nineteenth century anatomists, physicians and anthropologists continued to probe the mysteries of the face, its origins and the meaning of its expressions. If at first it seems unlikely that someone's character could be reflected in their appearance, then what about family inheritance? Appearance is decided at the moment of conception, and so are personality and talents that will emerge in adult life. To a certain extent character, abilities and tastes are also moulded by a person's environment and the influences he or she is subjected to.

Medicine and Magic

Eastern medicine and Western 'alternative' techniques are based on the idea that the mind and body are inextricably linked. Even those who practise conventional, orthodox methods are now accepting that how we think and feel affects our health. There is, too, growing evidence to suggest that the developing foetus is influenced by its mother's state of mind and emotional well-being. Indeed, one American organization is devoted to education before birth, and pregnant women spend hours every week talking to their unborn children, playing them classical music, and introducing them to family members in an apparently successful attempt to maximize intelligence.

Traditional Chinese medicine still uses a subtle and complex form of physiognomy in diagnosis – essentially this art is indistinguishable from that of the fortune-teller. Both healer and seer will have undergone the same rigorous training, the only difference is in the interpretation. To give you an idea of the basics of the Chinese Five Element Theory, the following is an outline of six basic types:

Element: Wood   Skin colour: Green   Organ: Liver

These people are well-built, with small hands and feet, and are hard-working. They are prone to imbalances of the liver.

Element: Fire   Skin colour: Red   Organ: Heart
Fire types have small heads and pointed chins. They are full of energy, make rash promises they cannot keep and are highly susceptible to flattery. Their hearts tend to be weak, and they are liable to suffer heart attacks if they do not take care of their health.

Element: Earth   Skin colour: Yellow   Organ: Spleen
Earth people have large heads, with round, fleshy faces. They are calm, generous, and not particularly ambitious.

Element: Metal   Skin colour: White   Organ: Lungs
Delicately-made with fine hands and feet, Metal types are straight-forward, meticulous and make excellent judges. They are credited with the power of clairvoyance and experience breathing difficulties and chest problems when under pressure.

Element: Water   Skin colour: Dark   Organ: Kidneys
Shadows under the eyes, a large head and abdomen and long spines belong to Water people. They may be over-fond of alcohol, and inhabit a fantasy world. Their kidneys, not helped by characteristic over-indulgence, are weak and will give trouble if the rest of the body is under severe stress.

This form of diagnosis is extremely subtle. Most of us are made up of a combination of elements – and the Chinese ideal is someone who is perfectly balanced in all of them. Excess or weakness in any of them is what, according to traditional belief, causes an imbalanced system – resulting in illness.

The typical skin colours belonging to each element are also not to be interpreted too literally – especially in the case of green-skinned Wood people. Rather, a highly-trained eye can detect a kind of cast or veil of colour which seems to hover about the face. Both East and West agree on a number of the preceding points, for most people know that a red-faced individual has got high blood pressure; dark rings below the eyes signal kidney trouble and looking a bit green reliably indicates an upset stomach.

Further investigation reveals interesting links between types of illness and character. Stress can cause symptoms ranging from palpitations to nausea and high blood pressure. Each person reacts to stress individually, and some even thrive under pressure. Research suggests that personality has a lot to do with it.

Science and Superstition

Palmistry is another branch of physiognomy, although nowadays it is studied and practised as a separate art. Yet it is based on similar foundations, for palmists say that you can read both character and the future by studying the lines on the hand.

Lines on the hand, claim palmists, are influenced by thoughts and feelings – an idea which many have dismissed as superstitious nonsense. Yet recent scientific discoveries show that a sizeable part of the brain is linked to the hands, while a further large section governs the face. Both the hands and face are concerned with the sending and receiving of information, rather like a radio station, as well as being highly sensitive parts of the anatomy.

If ancient teachings maintain that it is possible to predict what types of illness you are prone to long before you fall ill, then by taking steps early enough you may avoid the illness altogether. Little work has been done on facial analysis by Western scientists, but some thought-provoking studies carried out at the University of London have established links between palm patterns and inherited disorders. These conditions reveal themselves through specific kinds of line on the palm – often long before there are any more obvious symptoms. Of course, facial expressions constantly relay information. All over the world, scientists and psychologists are investigating their exact meanings. They have discovered some fleeting muscle movements called micro-expressions which are virtually invisible to the naked eye. Captured on film, they provide evidence of the intimate links between the physical and mental realms. Other research points to a two-way exchange between facial expression and mood. Positive expressions, even if forced, eventually cause a corresponding change of mood. Negative ones adversely affect well-being. Facial shape and structure are genetically determined along with colouring, skin type and so on. But a complex web of muscles covers the face, responding to every nuance of emotion. These responses may prove to have almost as much to do with overall appearance as inheritance. All muscles develop with use or waste away from neglect, and the face is no exception.

Such evidence suggests that, to an experienced eye, another face can be read like a book, for the body does seem to reflect the mind. By studying the art of face-reading, you will be able to make your own personal discoveries and decide for yourself just how accurate these beliefs can be.

Films, television, newspapers and magazines will all provide you with plenty of material for practice. Tread more cautiously when trying out your new physiognomy skills on family and friends, for it is easy to make mistakes and rash judgements. Choose your words carefully, too – most people, for instance, would rather hear that they are stubborn and determined than be told they are pig-headed types who cannot see another person's point of view. Above all, keep any negative or unpleasant discoveries to yourself – or you may become a very lonely expert indeed.

1

The Shape of the Face

When it comes to the shape of the face everyone is dipping into an astonishingly mixed bag. Genetic inheritance over the centuries determines a person's underlying facial structure, as well as colouring, skin type, height and so forth. You might look just like your father or mother, but you are just as likely to resemble a great-grandparent or a relative no-one even remembers.

The bone structure is the foundation upon which features are built. An experienced medical artist can create a recognizable face based upon a skull; but it can never be a totally accurate portrait because every face is also a complex network of muscles: as with the muscles in the rest of your body, facial muscles change shape with habitual tension or much-used expressions.

In addition, excess fat blurs the outline of a face, making it very hard to form anything but a rough impression. Many seriously overweight people are quite unrecognizable once they have shed those misleading extra pounds.

Chinese *Siang Mien* masters have isolated eleven types of face, which have poetic names such as Moon, Tree or Jade. Other, Western, experts suggest a minimum of six basic shapes – but there are countless variations. Generally speaking, human beings can be divided into two broad categories – those who are primarily mentally orientated, and those who are first and foremost practical people. Faces belonging to people who are happiest in the mental realms tend to be equally balanced – so that if you divided their faces into three, each section would measure roughly the same. Physical types tend to have larger jaws and shorter faces altogether.

Which is your face shape?

Your face should correspond to one of eight basic shapes. The shape of the face will give you an instant idea of the general character of those you know. However, though the face may be the mirror of the soul, it does not necessarily follow that a beautiful face mirrors a gracious spirit. Ugly people can be as good as angels, and those with captivating features may have evil characters. Great literature abounds with generous characters with bizarre or unattractive looks. Our faces, like our lives, are made up of contradictions.

To read a face, you first have to consider it as a whole. Then, like a caricaturist, you should concentrate on the individual feature (forehead, eyebrows, eyes, nose, mouth, ears, cheek-bones or chin) that first attracts your attention. Then you must decide whether the striking feature, such as a large nose, is in harmony with the rest of the face. If, despite its disproportionate size, it is compatible with the rest of the face, then you have discovered the first positive element of the face. A part can be in harmony even when it contrasts with other parts, as long as overall it somehow looks right. A large nose will be compatible with the rest of the face if at least two other features, such as the ears and chin, are prominent. If the nose is the only discordant feature, it may indicate negative characteristics. However, at the beginning of any analysis all of your judgements should be speculative. Only when you have covered all the aspects involved in studying a face can you start to draw conclusions about someone's character. This is not necessarily a difficult or slow process, as in everybody's face there are some very clear signs. Four signs, according to Chinese physiognomy, are always positive: a wide forehead; a thin nose with fleshy nostrils; fine ears with pronounced lobes and a rounded chin. If two or more of these characteristics are present in a face, you can be sure that it belongs to a person who is bound to succeed in life.

Round face
This face has a strong bone structure but is not necessarily fat. It denotes intense mental activity, resistance to illness and self-confidence. It can indicate laziness. These people generally have long lives.

Diamond face
A narrow forehead, prominent cheek-bones and a pointed chin belong to a person who is generally warm, endowed with a strong will and lucky in their career. It can sometimes indicate egoism and unscrupulousness.

Rectangular face
A face which gives the impression of being longer than it is broad, with an ample forehead and barely visible cheek-bones, denotes creativity, intelligence and self-control. It can be a sign of infidelity.

Square face
A wide forehead and jawbone and a sturdy bone structure denote a stable character which is honest and well-balanced. It is the face of a person who is used to making decisions, and is common among politicians and statesmen. They may marry more than once, and are passionate lovers.

Triangular face
The combination of a wide forehead, prominent cheek-bones and a pointed chin, generally with thin lips, are signs of a brilliant and sensual temperament, intelligence and ambition. This face belongs to great seductresses and queens.

Wide jaw and a narrower forehead
Here the forehead is narrower than the jaw, the mouth and nose generally small. In men, this indicates physical strength and competitiveness, in women a tendency to take command and the ability to make a career.

Wide forehead and a square chin
A wide forehead, full lips and a square chin indicate balance, astuteness and creativity. A long, successful life and inner peace will probably be yours if you have this face.

Prominent cheekbones
The irregular features of a prominent forehead, cheek-bones and chin denote strength of character, perseverance, energy and the ability to pick oneself up again after a setback. Such features can also indicate egocentricity and lack of generosity.

Round face

The first of the eight principal types into which the age-old Chinese science of physiognomy divided the human face is the round face. It is not the most common face shape, but it reveals some very distinct characteristics.

It is not enough just to take into account the shape when deciding whether a face belongs to the round category. There are faces which look round simply because they are too fat, and faces which appear to be round because the chin is under-developed or the forehead is receding. The true round face has a sturdy bone structure, a wide, convex forehead, high, flat cheek-bones, flat ears, a wide nose, a well-defined mouth and thin lips. A round face, whilst not fat, tends to be fleshy. This person generally prefers mental to physical activity, but can behave differently according to circumstances. The owner of a round face can also be very enterprising and have many surprises up his or her sleeve. Almost all the Chinese emperors had a round face; so did some great explorers and many privateers.

People with round faces are quick-witted and readily adapt to any situation. They also have a keen intellect, generally reaching the peak of their abilities in their forties. Before then, it is as if they are steadily preparing themselves for the time when their full potential will be realized. Round-faced people generally live to a ripe old age. The orientals say of them that they are not even in a hurry to die.

Those who also have a long, thin neck have great resistance to illness. In love, they are sincere, but often erotic desires lead them to infidelity.

The former American president, John F. Kennedy, wrote in a famous letter to his brother, Robert, that in politics, people with round faces are intelligent, but untrustworthy, interlocutors. He was referring to Nikita Kruschev and, probably, to Mao-Tse-Tung. He trusted Pope John XXIII, who only had a *seemingly* round face because of its fleshiness, unconditionally. However, this may also have had much to do with the fact that Kennedy was a Catholic.

Both the modern model (above) and Guillaume des Ursins (left), present typical examples of round faces

Diamond face

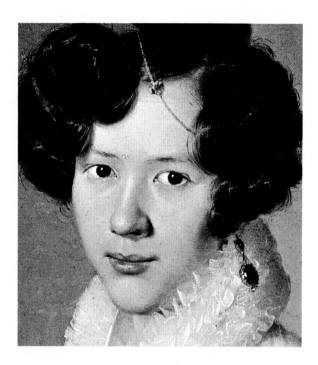

Two determined female diamond faces

The diamond face is easily recognizable and belongs to countless stage stars, famous women and courageous warriors. This face is narrow at the top of the forehead, with prominent cheek-bones and a pointed chin.

The Chinese consider it lucky if, on leaving home for an important meeting, they meet a man or woman with a diamond face. If the face belongs to a woman, it means that the meeting will bring lasting fruits of success, and if it belongs to a man, it portends immediate, rather than long-term, business success. People with this face are generally lucky in love and have great resistance to illness. They are remarkably ambitious and have a keen sense of humour.

This type of face is usually accompanied by a regular nose, a thin, well-defined mouth and flat ears. However, women with a diamond-shaped face often have full lips. If they do, some of their typical and more annoying characteristics may be exaggerated, especially ambition and the desire to assert themselves publicly.

Many diamond-faced people are dissatisfied during adolescence and youth, and only find fulfilment in the latter half of their lives. They remember the difficulties they have overcome to the end of their lives. The School of Physiognomy in Los Angeles, California, which liaises with many of the Oriental schools of physiognomy, has proved statistically that this type of face belongs to at least 60 per cent of self-made men.

A person with a diamond face is also a good fighter, both physically and mentally. Several boxers have this type of face, and it is said that the Chinese emperors chose warriors for the front line from among those with diamond-shaped faces. Napoleon, too, had many generals with such a face shape.

Those with this face must beware of becoming unpopular, and of the intense psychological suffering which unpopularity causes them. They must therefore try to maintain good relations with those useful to them at work, and fight the outbursts of intolerance to which they are prone. People with this type of face who are destined for greatest success in life have very pronounced typical features – cheeks which recede below the cheek-bones and a decidedly pointed chin. A prominent nose, on the other hand, is a sign of lack of control and of greed: these are the impulses which the owner of this face must always remember to curb.

Rectangular face

The Chinese call the rectangular face a tree-face, because it is like a tree trunk in shape. The sides are vertical, the ears are generally flat, the cheek-bones visible but not prominent, the mouth well-defined and the chin fleshy. It is similar to a diamond face, without the high cheek-bones.

This face often has a pithy or irregular surface, patches where the skin texture or colouring stands out. This gives the face a highly expressive character. The Chinese say that the tree-face speaks for itself, mirroring the turmoils of the soul.

The rectangular face belongs to people who are prone to introspection and sometimes aggression. They have tremendous self-control and master their feelings to the point of repressing them. They are creative and are lucky to be able to fall back on unexpected resources. In the Chinese imagination, this is symbolically represented by trees which, every spring, burst into new leaf.

Those with this face develop typical characteristics at various stages of their lives. Their youth lasts a long time, and they move into maturity with no loss of energy. Many rectangular-faced people are at their best at a mature age.

They are committed to their jobs, which they put before domestic commitments, and sometimes this can cause problems in their family life. Worse problems arise if they feel bored or trapped.

Living with someone with this face is not easy, but a relationship can be very rewarding if you can accept his or her natural role as boss. These people have more good qualities than defects, and are fundamentally creative, resilient, reliable and hard working.

Chinese experts say rectangular faces resemble tree-trunks. Like trees, their owners have long lives and improve with age

Square face

Politicians and diplomats often have this type of face, and, almost exclusively, it belongs to men. The structure and shape of the face are usually immediately obvious.

A square face is a sign of incorruptibility in public affairs. It is also a sign of impulsiveness and, sometimes, obstinacy. Men with this type of face will make up their minds and keep to their decisions, even at the cost of being unpopular. They are passionate and generally unfaithful in love because they cannot resist the fascination of an affair. It is common for men with this face to marry several times.

Generosity is perhaps the most marked trait of the square-faced person. He or she does not inspire confidence at first but will always prove to be a willing and affectionate friend. He or she puts his or her friends first in everything, and demands from them fidelity and submissiveness. In exchange he or she offers protection, but beware – this person is capable of unexpected outbursts.

Winston Churchill had a square face; another famous person with a square face was the Count of Cavour, whose brilliance as a politician and statesman are legendary. Few knew of his countless affairs in his private life.

Those with a square face have a high opinion of themselves. In arguments, they tend to force their own viewpoint, and it is best not to contradict them for they genuinely believe they are right. However, any ill humour is generally short-lived.

Women with this face have similar characteristics to the men, except they differ emotionally: the woman is almost always a good wife and mother, and generally represses the desire to be unfaithful. However, if she comes into conflict with her partner, she may not only want to recover her independence, but also want to avoid another binding relationship.

Square-faced people, both male and female, are favoured by good fortune and a long life.

Triangular face

This type of face is typical of the world's great seducers and seductresses. It reveals a restless spirit and, sometimes, emotional fragility: it takes sensitivity to live peacefully with a triangular-faced person.

A wide forehead, high, prominent cheek-bones, a well-defined mouth and a pointed chin are the main features of triangular faces. Endowed with a lively temperament, a keen intelligence and marked sensuality, individuals who have this type of face are ambitious and tend to stand out socially. Many great seductresses throughout history – Mary Tudor and Elizabeth of Austria, for example – had beautiful triangular-shaped faces; so do many screen stars, such as Marlene Dietrich, Pier Angeli and Elizabeth Taylor. However, for all their charisma, these men and women are often unhappy in love.

Those with this face shape are close to their families, but they tend to free themselves from family life in order to follow their own inclinations. Any inner conflict this causes them can, in some cases, influence their character. Triangular-faced people are always justifying themselves, and can become exasperated and exasperating because of this. They frequently find it hard to understand their own motives.

In their love lives, these people are inconstant. Attracted by new experiences and encouraged by successful relationships with the opposite sex, they often make difficult partners. To live peacefully with them you have constantly to change and support them in their desire for novelty. Sometimes it takes little to appease their anxieties. Do not oppose any decision they make to go on a trip, change jobs, or escape from daily routine, which they find oppressive.

In most cases, this type of face goes with a tall, slim, attractive physique. People with this face may not actually be tall, but because they are well proportioned they seem so. They can use this asset to gain popularity in the public eye, and do well in jobs which involve contact with the general public. In the seventies, certain major airline companies preferred to choose air hostesses who had triangular-shaped faces.

These people make up their minds on the spur of the moment and find it hard to change them. You should remember this whenever you present them with a problem. Their main weakness is an underlying nervous fragility. Sometimes, for no particular reason, they become depressed and lose faith. They enjoy the attentions of others – in the words of Elizabeth of Austria, 'More than respected, I wish to be appreciated. And I do not hate flattery.' Indeed, if you give them plenty of attention it will help lift their periodic fits of gloom.

Elizabeth of Austria (left) enjoyed attention, and honestly admitted her fondness for flattery. Capricious triangular-faced people all share this tendency

Wide jaw and narrower forehead

This type of face has a wide, square jaw, a fairly wide forehead and long, broad wrinkles. The Chinese associate this face with the earth, because it is characteristically well defined and changes little. A person with this face will tend to be aggressive and touchy; when he or she has taken a decision he or she will want to see it through to the end, regardless of any obstacles (including people) in his or her way. People with this type of face fight to the very last to stand by their decisions, especially in their emotional life. One of the most famous 'earth-faced' people in history was Henry VIII. In order to marry the woman he pleased, he not only repudiated his legitimate wife, but, in doing so, defied the authority of the Church.

People with this face love success. They choose partners with similar characteristics to themselves, and will always achieve the goals they set themselves. A good example of a woman with this face shape is Jacqueline Kennedy – a woman with almost unparalleled determination to succeed and to assert her own personality even at the most difficult times. After the assassination of her husband, President John F. Kennedy, she married the

Greek millionaire Aristotle Onassis, thereby defying the public opinion of half the world, which preferred to make her into a symbol of inconsolable grief. The Chinese say, 'There are two things which it is impossible to prevent: horses from whinnying when they have decided to whinny and earth-faces from marrying when they have decided to get married'.

Compared with the strength it signifies, this face has fine features. The nose, in particular, is small and pointed and the lips are thin. Jacqueline Kennedy is an exception: her nose is too prominent to be in harmony with the rest of her face, and her mouth is too big. Such discordant features create an impression of irregularity, but at the same time make her face interesting.

A man with this face is not always a perfect father. He has difficulty in communicating with his children and tends not to follow their progress. On the other hand, his sons will respect his strength and authority and he can easily gain their gratitude and admiration. Those with this face like money and all that it can bring. If they find fulfilment in life they can be very generous in return.

Jacqueline Kennedy's irregular, but highly-attractive earth face captivated two of the world's most powerful and famous men

Wide forehead and a square chin

Astute and intelligent, those who have this type of face commit themselves totally to achieving their goals. They become ruthlessly determined once they see the opportunity to assert themselves through work or improve their social position.

The distinctive features of this face are a wide forehead, well-defined mouth, full lips, and a square chin. These indicate stability, astuteness and, usually, a long life. Those with this face often become public figures. Pablo Picasso, Joseph Stalin, the actors Jean-Paul Belmondo and Paul Newman all had or have faces with a wide forehead and a square chin.

Among women, Jane Fonda, Meryl Streep, and Queen Maria-Theresa of Austria have or had this face shape. Vitality, enterprise and a positive, but difficult, character belong to those with this face.

Both men and women of this type tend to be attention seeking. They live from day to day, seizing and taking advantage of every opportunity life offers. Their lives are full of periods of intense activity and periods of waiting. In their relationships they are generally courteous, but find it difficult to make true friends. Always tense and always trying to assert themselves, they lack spontaneity. In love they are kind, but selfish, and therefore do not hesitate to break strong ties when it comes to improving their career or social position.

These people are endowed with great courage for physical feats. Many parachutists and animal tamers have this type of face, for example. On the other hand, they do not like wasting energy on secondary objectives, which is why they can sometimes seem detached and lacking in interest. This can create trouble in their relationships; others are often uncertain about the depth of their feelings.

Those with this face attain full intellectual maturity as they reach full physical maturity; many artists with this type of face make their impact after the age of forty. Destined for a long life, it is as if they save their energy for important occasions – as Picasso said, 'When it is time, I'll show the world how well I can paint. For the time being, I prefer to keep practising.'

Those with a wide forehead and square chin have a way with words. They are calm and can be obstinate, but sometimes the opposite is also true: if they realize they cannot achieve a goal, they quietly withdraw and begin to think of a way round it. Other ambivalent characteristics come to the fore at times, as their choices depend very much on the circumstances they are in at the time.

Jean-Paul Belmondo's nose reveals his early career as a boxer, while the model's face shape (below) shows determination

Prominent cheek-bones

Christopher Columbus; an inspired and tenacious explorer

This face is easy to recognize, and the character of its owner is equally distinct. In women, it is often a sign of inconstancy in love.

A wide forehead and prominent cheek-bones are the salient features of this face, which overall is both solid and bony. The main qualities of the owners of this face are strength of character, perseverance, mental energy and the ability to pick themselves up after a setback. Their chief faults are egocentricity and, sometimes, lack of generosity.

Their features appear to be irregular, but, if you observe them carefully, you will see they are harmonious. The impression of irregularity is created by the extreme mobility of the skin tissue. The complexion is usually pale and the intensity of the expression in the eyes is often alert and penetrating.

Famous examples of people with this face are Christopher Columbus, Charlemagne, Lawrence the Magnificent, Walter Scott, Edward Kennedy, General Rommel, Greta Garbo, Julie Christie and Faye Dunaway. Giuseppe Verdi and Ludwig van Beethoven had very marked characteristics.

People with this type of face are very often leaders, but this face may also belong to less noble adventurers such as spies and criminals.

Many men who have made their own fortune (producer Mike Todd, for example, a former husband of Elizabeth Taylor), are fine examples of those with this face. Inconstant and restless, they find it hard to be faithful husbands. Women with this type of face are similarly inconstant in their affections. Both sexes tend to take charge and like flattery.

These people love to live fully. They know what they like and stick to it, and are reluctant to change their habits, preferences and activities. To live happily with such people, you must be supportive and always retain a very balanced view of events. Most importantly, you must not go against their decisions: it is only possible to make them change their minds by using a great deal of tact.

Former film-star, Greta Garbo, became equally famous during her self-imposed exile from the world

Animal faces

Wolves, pigs, silly cows and lion-hearted heroes are all part of our everyday vocabulary, but all these animal analogies stem from ancient Greek and Roman physiognomy. Animal characteristics – both physical and mental – were related to human character analysis. It is hard to say how much scientific validity these ideas have, but it can be enjoyable to see how many types you notice on public transport or at a party. Even if these old ideas can be dismissed as fanciful nonsense, people still tend to use them when trying to describe someone's face or personality, as numerous common sayings reveal. The following are twelve major types and their characteristics:

Creature	Name	Positive	Negative
Lion	Leonine	Strong, generous	Proud, rash
Cat	Feline	Loving, kind	Jealous, selfish
Dog	Canine	Faithful, wise	Docile
Horse	Equine	Loyal, brave	Proud, austere
Sheep	Ovine	Gentle, sincere	Prudish, timid
Ox	Bovine	Firm, sensual	Complacent, self-indulgent
Bear	Ursine	Decisive, clever	Bad-tempered
Pig	Porcine	Shrewd, amorous	Vindictive, insincere
Donkey	Asinine	Content, practical	Lazy, coarse
Wolf	Lupine	Ambitious, flexible	Cruel, melancholy
Fish	Ichthyine	Industrious, active	Vain, secretive
Eagle	Aquiline	Bold, courageous	Egotistical

King Faisal's beak-like nose dominates his face. The Ancient Greeks would have likened these features to an eagle's

Cosmic characters

Astrology is another centuries-old way of classifying physical types and their personalities. Certain planetary influences – not necessarily the birth-sign itself – appear to affect our appearance. This may seem unbelievable, but recent German research does suggest that it is true. Edith Wangemann's investigations reveal that some aspects, or relationships, between the planets in the birth chart influence our appearance.

Without delving too deeply into the mysteries and complexities of astrology, it is interesting to try to group people into planetary types and see if their personalities fit into the picture.

Astrology has long credited the planet with an influence upon appearance. Recent research suggests this could be true

Sign: Aries, 21 March – 21 April
Planet: Mars

Description: Reddish hair, strong limbs, muscular, long broad face, aquiline nose, bright lively eyes, marked eyebrows.
Character: Martian types are ambitious, quick-tempered, full of nervous energy which makes them restless. They are also astonishingly selfish and honest.

Sign: Taurus, 21 April – 22 May
Planet: Venus

Description: Short to medium height, rounded body, full face and throat, generous mouth, large eyes, often very attractive.
Character: Love of security, practicality and stubbornness are all typical attributes. These people love beautiful things, are sensual, good-hearted and patient.

Sign: Gemini, 22 May – 22 June
Planet: Mercury

Description: Tall and slim, with a tendency to be dark, Mercurial types have angular, oval faces, narrow foreheads and chins. Their eyes sparkle with amusement, and are usually dark or hazel in colour.
Character: Versatile, talkative, indecisive and impatient. Mercurial characters move quickly both mentally and physically, and may scatter their considerable energy in too many different directions. They are talented liars, witty and tactful.

Sign: Cancer, 22 June – 23 July
Planet: Moon

Description: Broad, rounded faces with full cheeks and large, usually grey, eyes belong to Lunar people. Not normally tall, they are well-made with full stomachs and slender arms.
Character: Dreamy, sensitive and moody Lunar personalities are often artistic. They hate change, and need lots of affection in their relationships. Great worriers, they will always have a little money put aside for a rainy day.

Sign: Leo, 23 July – 24 August
Planet: Sun

Description: Tall or medium-sized Solar people have fresh complexions, oval faces and large, penetrating eyes.

Their voices are clear and strong, noses straight, and shoulders broad. They move in a deliberate, slow way and are often blonde or red-haired.
Character: Extrovert, generous and enthusiastic, Sun types also tend to be vain and proud. Nothing eclipses them for long, for they are blessed with a lot of energy and a great appetite for life. They love entertaining and being entertained and are usually popular.

Sign: Virgo, 24 August – 23 September
Planet: Mercury

Description: These types are nicely-proportioned, with a medium-sized body, clear, warm complexion, broad forehead and delicate features. They are usually slim and attractive, with brown hair and round heads. Their eyes are characterized by a gentle, reserved expression.
Character: Cautious, shy, and fastidious, these people are also great worriers. They have delicate stomachs, and are often very interested in special diets. They work well in teams, and are both conscientious and painstaking. Usually quiet and polite, they are highly analytical and articulate once you get to know them.

Sign: Libra, 23 September – 23 October
Planet: Venus

Description: Typically fairly tall, with beautiful bodies, these people often give a feminine impression whether male or female. The complexion is fine and clear, with dimples or a cleft chin. Both eyes and nose are well-formed, and there is always something pleasant about their appearance.
Character: Very charming and affectionate, these people hate being alone. Pleasure-loving and sociable, they need peaceful surroundings and cannot take too much pressure. They can be very romantic and artistic – but also fickle, dependent and lazy.

Sign: Scorpio, 23 October – 23 November
Planet: Pluto/Mars

Description: Broad faces with thick necks, magnetic, often dark, eyes, and a strong, broad-shouldered body. There are two types: those with swarthy complexions and dark hair, and those with pale faces with sandy hair and penetrating grey eyes. Whether tall or short, there is always a feeling of strength about them.
Character: Forceful, secretive and moody, these people are also often highly intuitive and emotional. Their inscrutable nature hides a hot-blooded, passionate personality – and they can be extremely jealous and vindictive when crossed. They work hard, and usually achieve their aims in life.

Sign: Sagittarius, 23 November – 22 December
Planet: Jupiter

Description: Fresh, sometimes ruddy complexions, long faces with high foreheads, and Grecian noses belong to Jupiterian, or Jovial, types. They are strong, often tall, and have clear blue or brown eyes with a steady gaze. The men tend to go bald early, and if tall may stoop.
Character: Outgoing and freedom-loving, Jovial people are also philosophical and restless. They may prove unreliable and tactless – without meaning to be – and have a good sense of humour. They enjoy travel, are untidy, and like a varied social life.

Sign: Capricorn, 22 December – 21 January
Planet: Saturn

Description: Tall, slim and bony with dark hair and pale, sallow complexions. They often have prominent noses or cheekbones, long necks and narrow chins. They do not move very quickly, but every action is measured and deliberate.
Character: Serious, introverted and ambitious Saturnine people have a strong sense of duty. They are loyal and patient – but find it hard to have fun and so are often lonely in life. A high regard for money leads them to spend sensibly and mistrust extravagance in others.

Sign: Aquarius, 21 January – 19 February
Planet: Saturn/Uranus

Description: Tall, robust and healthy with a delicate, dry-skinned complexion. They have long faces with narrow chins and are often fair-haired. The eyes are clear and seem to be focused on the far horizon.
Character: Idealistic, sociable, and somewhat detached, these people may have many superficial friendships, but few deep ones – although they are always willing to help others. They are eccentric, work well in teams, are often intellectual and independent.

Sign: Pisces, 19 February – 20 March
Planet: Neptune/Jupiter

Description: Short, with long lean faces and pale complexions, Neptunian types can incline to puffiness due to water retention. Their light-coloured eyes have a sleepy or watery look. They may be clumsy, or move in an unco-ordinated, nervous way.
Character: Highly imaginative, reserved, and emotional, Neptunian types are also sensitive, self-sacrificing and intuitive. They can be visionaries, striving to create a better world, or they may descend into the depths of addiction to drink and drugs.

2

Areas of the Face

In this chapter, the face is divided into three main sections: from the forehead to the eyebrows; from the eyebrows to the tip of the nose and from the nose tip to the chin. In China, these sections are believed to correspond to the three ages of man – the forehead represents youth (from fifteen to thirty); the centre of the face tells what kind of middle age you can expect; while 'old age' begins early by Western standards, at fifty – and is symbolized by the area from the nose tip to the chin. By closely observing individual features an expert can not only analyse character, but also make predictions for the future. The forehead, eye area and nose are further subdivided into eight regions said to represent all life's major concerns.

Western experts prefer to concentrate on detailed character analysis. They equate the forehead with intelligence, critical faculties, and stability. The popular terms 'broad-minded' and 'narrow-minded' have their roots in physiognomy: a narrow forehead is said to signal a cramped view of life, while a sweeping brow reveals someone who is prepared to accept a wide range of ideas and beliefs.

Eyes and mouths are perhaps the most significant features of all, and close attention must be given not only to their shape but also to their expression. A pair of large, delicately-shaped eyes may be dull and cloudy – indicating tiredness, ill-health or perhaps depression. A generous, full mouth may turn down at the corners – here is someone who is probably lively and sensual, but sulky too.

Indeed, the old saying, 'Don't pull that face or you'll stick like it' still holds some truth. After the age of about twenty-five, the habitual use of facial muscles begins to show – so that even the most beautiful or handsome face in the world will not be able to hide an underlying unpleasant personality forever.

The three main areas of the face

'You can know a man from his appearance and you can tell a judicious man from his face', goes a famous Biblical saying. However, it is not always possible to tell a person's character without carefully observing all the components of their face. The expression, the smile and the eyes reveal the nature of the soul, but often a first impression of a face depends on the psychological state of the individual we are observing. This state may only be temporary and is determined by a wide variety of circumstances. The science of physiognomy enables you to go beyond first impressions by taking into account as well the body structure. This makes it possible to form a detailed and, generally, very accurate 'diagnosis'.

The face is divided into three zones, the forehead, nose and chin areas. Each area corresponds to a major facet of the personality. The forehead area goes from the hairline (the hairline is the point where the hair begins – or began when there was hair) to the top of the nose. The nose area falls from the top to the bottom of the nose. The chin area extends from the base of the nose to the base of the chin.

Each of these three zones relates to an aspect of the personality. The forehead area, or upper area, reflects the intellect. The nose area, or central area, reflects sensibility. The chin area, or lower area, reflects the instincts. In a truly harmonious face, these three areas are perfectly proportioned. None of them, even on close observation, should

1. This zone corresponds to mental characteristics; its size and shape indicate whether someone is primarily intellectual, or creative

2. The middle zone is linked with the feelings. Prominence in this area reveals pronounced emotions

3. Nose to chin reflects instinct, will, and the roots of the personality

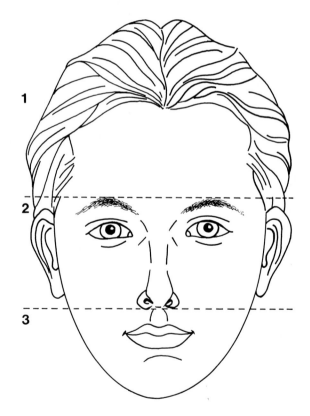

This woman's strong jawline suggests a strong-willed character. Her well-defined nose indicates that her heart rules her head

stand out more than the others. If one of the areas does stand out, as in the majority of cases, the corresponding characteristics are accentuated.

Before embarking on the study of the forehead area, you must remember that the characteristics revealed in your study must be considered both in conjunction with the other areas of the face and in conjunction with the various parts of the body.

Predominant forehead or upper area
This indicates rationality, lucidity and, usually, great intellectual strength.

Predominant nose or middle area
This reveals emotiveness, sentimentality and irrationality.

Predominant chin or lower area
This is a sign of instinctiveness, common sense and a strong will.

The forehead

By examining the various characteristics of the forehead, you can discover a person's intellectual and moral qualities. The forehead tells you about a person's mind and his or her way of conceptualizing existence. A balanced psyche can be detected by measuring the height of the forehead, which should be equal to the central and lower areas of the face.

The forehead is subdivided into three parts, the upper part (near the roots of the hair), the central part (in the middle) and the lower part (down to the eyebrows). If the upper part of the forehead is particularly pronounced, it is an indication of noble sentiments and generosity. If the central part is prominent, it denotes common sense and security. If the lower part protrudes more than the other parts, it reveals a sense of realism and sensuality.

High forehead
This reveals intelligence, broadmindedness and the ability to concentrate and think laterally. If there is a distinct disproportion in relation to the rest of the face (far more than a third) this individual is very detached from real problems.

Wide forehead
If there is a width of more than 12 cm from one temple to the other, this indicates a remarkable ability to assimilate information, a good memory and a craving for learning and knowledge. It also indicates a changeable character and sensuality.

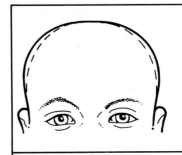

A wide, high forehead signals breadth of vision, leadership qualities, and a practical approach to problems

An egg-shaped brow reveals intelligence and creativity, but sometimes such people have their head in the clouds

High and wide forehead
This shows a logical mind, an instinct for leadership, constancy and original thinking.

Low forehead
A forehead which is less than 6 cm high reveals a sense of reality, a desire to earn money and utilitarianism.

This self-portrait by M. Quentin de la Tour shows the high, wide forehead associated with an original, logical mind

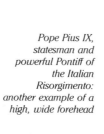

Pope Pius IX, statesman and powerful Pontiff of the Italian Risorgimento: another example of a high, wide forehead

Queen Victoria's low, slightly protruding brow reveals her strong, sometimes stubborn nature. A prominent ridge above the eyebrows suggests energy and dynamism

Narrow forehead
If a forehead is less than 12 cm wide this person has analytical intelligence and is likely to take an almost obsessive interest in a hobby, pastime or sport.

High narrow forehead
This reveals an ability to carry out ideas and original inventions. It also shows egocentricity.

Very prominent forehead
This is a sign of a strong and persevering person who sees his or her own initiatives through. An ability to understand others and to devote himself or herself to the common good belongs to this person.

Forehead with numerous bulges
The owner of this forehead is highly active and dynamic, with a passionate, sometimes violent, temperament.

Straight perpendicular forehead
A forehead like this reveals a decisive and secure character who craves freedom, and grasps opportunities.

Concave forehead
This reveals psychological problems; uncertainty and fears can delay development.

Square forehead
A forehead like this is a sign of a mathematical, coherent and precise mind, and of someone with great faith in his or her own abilities.

Elongated, oval forehead
This shows an artistic temperament, which is drawn towards mysticism.

Backward sloping forehead
This is a sign of a powerful imagination, eloquence, emotiveness and, sometimes, geniality.

Forehead slightly sloping backwards
This reveals common sense and sensitivity.

Bony forehead
This person has a receptive but disorganized and very nervous temperament.

The eyes

It is through the expression in the eyes that human beings express states of mind and convey their innermost private feelings. They are the most expressive part of the face and the windows to the soul. In the clarity or the obscurity of a gaze man reveals or betrays his qualities and defects. People who have something to hide or a complex they wish to disguise prefer not to look the person opposite them in the eyes, while those who are able to open themselves up completely and wish to get to know others well look straight into the eyes of the person they are talking to. Physiognomy reveals many more aspects of the personality through a study of the eyes.

These large but deep-set eyes reflect an observant, critical and sometimes moody nature

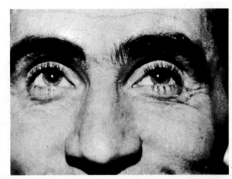

Ava Gardner's slender, arched eyebrows signal a restless, active personality

Walter Chiari's elongated eyebrows, reaching the temples, denote a reckless streak and someone who scatters his energy

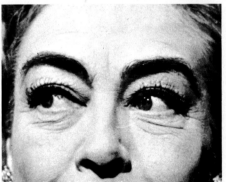

Hollywood legend, Joan Crawford, has powerful, well-marked eyebrows. They reveal a love of success and an indomitable spirit

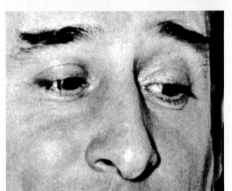

Someone with short, straight eyebrows, like Italian comedian Renata Racel, is often methodical, critical and pedantic

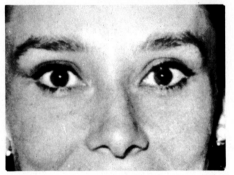

These widely-spaced eyebrows belong to actress Audrey Hepburn, indicating a warm, happy temperament

Handsome actor, Gregory Peck, illustrates the heavy brows of a tenacious, decisive individual

Big eyes

Large, luminous eyes indicate a combative, exuberant nature which burns up energy, often in frantic activity. Large, soft, velvety eyes reveal a romantic, dreamy nature. In general, large eyes denote an aesthetic sense, imagination and good powers of observation.

Very big eyes

Extraordinarily large eyes belong to people endowed with a deep inner life but who are not always able fully to express their own thoughts and feelings. They also tend to waste time in diverse activities to which they are not necessarily suited. Only when they meet someone able to give them objective advice do they succeed in giving the best of themselves.

Small eyes

These eyes are typical of a lively, curious nature which is interested in many things. Their owners may be unfaithful in love due to their constant thirst for new experiences. Small eyes also denote shrewdness, enterprise and keen intelligence. Sometimes people with small eyes become impatient and lose an objective view of events, but their vitality makes up for their errors of judgement.

Very small eyes

A tendency to take a personal view of things belongs to this person. The subject is attracted above all to things which arouse his or her sensuality, and also desires material success. Very small eyes can be a sign of selfishness and ambition.

Protruding eyes

Such eyes reveal a communicative and hot-tempered extrovert. Protruding eyes are often fascinating and have a magnetic force. They are also a sign of exhibitionism, vanity and a vivid imagination. Medically, they can indicate thyroid problems which in turn can explain the subject's quick mood changes, irritability and temporary bouts of depression.

Deep set eyes

Deep set eyes reflect an observant, critical nature. Their owners are prone to nervous exhaustion and like to isolate themselves in order to analyse their own feelings and enrich their inner world. They find it difficult to express their own thoughts clearly.

Round eyes

If the eyes are clear and alert, this person has an enterprising and decisive nature. If they are slightly cloudy, they express a talented, spontaneous and happy nature which succeeds in fascinating the opposite sex.

Almond eyes

If the expression in these eyes is cold, it reveals astuteness and a fairly calculating nature. If it is warm, it indicates a capacity for self-control, as well as hidden sensuality. Almond eyes are also a sign of an inclination towards an artistic career.

Half-closed eyes

When the eyelids are slightly lowered, it is a sign of a withdrawn character who tends to be sceptical. It conveys shyness, pride, jealousy in the subject's private life and rebellion against convention.

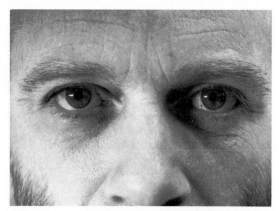

Large, deep-set eyes denote an artistic, observant and thoughtful character. Nervous exhaustion could be a problem

Almond eyes belong to creative, self-controlled but sensual people. Here a warm expression masks an astute personality

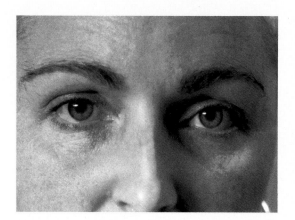

Wide-apart eyes and eyebrows indicate honesty, idealism and an optimistic approach to life

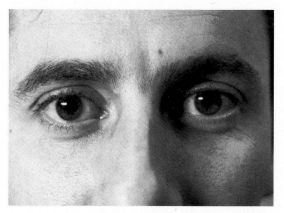

Rounded, appealing eyes suggest talent and enterprise. A fraction of white visible below the iris shows great sensitivity

This Oriental girl's naturally slanting eyes are wide apart and sparkling, suggesting vitality and humour. Full lower lids denote a warm, likeable personality

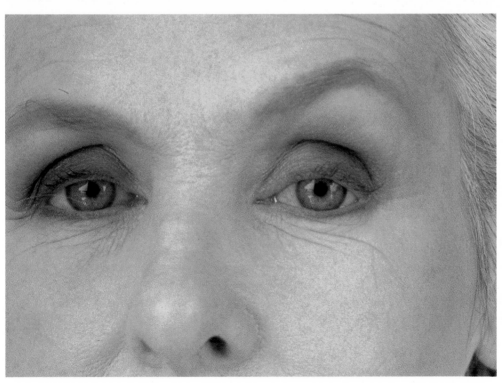

Eyes tend to become more deep-set as we get older. Here, heavy upper lids and large eyes show natural exuberance tempered by maturity

The nose

If the eyes are the windows of the soul, it is the nose which is one of the most obvious clues to temperament and personality. In any face, the nose is one of the first elements that the observer perceives and classifies. A pair of not particularly bright eyes, an imperfect mouth or a jutting chin are less obvious than a nose which is too distinctive. In plastic surgery, more than half the operations are on noses, and, often, the patient with a modified nose subsequently regains confidence and his or her attitude towards life changes for the better.

Opinion about what is the perfect nose has changed several times over the years. Not long ago, for example, a tiny turned-up nose was generally admired in women. Today, this type of nose is considered too affected, and a medium-sized well-defined nose is fashionable. In the future, Greek, Roman or Oriental noses might become the aesthetic ideal. The study of the face is not influenced by trends or changes to the nose caused by plastic surgery. Physiognomy must deal with the *natural* size and shape of the nose in order to define aspects of character.

Long nose
A long nose denotes a strong personality and an urge to make one's authority felt. This character is ambitious, proud and sensitive. He or she can be generous, but only towards those who show gratitude. Statistics confirm that most people who are good at asserting themselves have long noses. They have 'good noses' for business and shine in the artistic sphere and in their relationships with others as well. Overall they have good powers of intuition.

Small nose
This belongs to imaginative and talented people who are always seeking new sensations and who sometimes act on the spur of the moment. They have a childish side to their character which comes out in naive idealism or in unpredictable outbursts of anger. They want to do everything in a hurry and without thinking too hard. They are often influenced by others' opinions.

Broad nose
A large nose which is broad at the base is a sign of an active, optimistic and sensual nature. Such people are capable of great enthusiasm and know how to enjoy life in every way. Sometimes, in search of pleasure, they forget some of their moral principles, but they never go beyond certain limits. They are reliable and efficient at work.

Thin nose
A refined, delicate temperament is indicated by this nose. These subjects possess good aesthetic judgement and psychological intuition. They also have a few minor defects: they can be selfish, and habitually work out every situation to their own advantage, but they always move with astuteness and tact. Their moods are fluctuating and they are easily influenced.

Squashed nose
If the nose is squashed as the result of a fall or practising a sport, as in the case of many boxers, it cannot form the basis of a physiognomical examination. If, however, a

Small noses belong to impatient sensation-seekers. Here, a slight curve indicates inner conflict and introversion

A broad, full nose denotes a pleasure-loving nature. Straightness reveals a good decision-maker

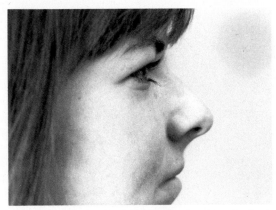

A small rounded nose shows imaginative, impetuous tendencies. This person could prove unpredictable at times

Leonardo da Vinci's sketch of Dante illustrates a pronounced nose, indicating strength of character and earthy sensuality

person is born with this type of nose, it indicates an instinctive, sensual and impressionable temperament. In many cases, a squashed nose also denotes insecurity and superficiality. As the subject matures, he or she will become loved for the kindness and warmth he or she is capable of arousing.

Aquiline nose

This reveals a well-defined personality which does not easily adapt to the demands of others. This person tends to dominate situations, and if this is not immediately possible, he or she prefers to wait for the right moment. He or she has a nervous, imaginative, intelligent and creative temperament. For this person, the search for a harmonious love life is not easy.

Pointed nose

If the nose has a sharp point it reveals a curious, probing character. If the sharp tip is accompanied by a thin nose,

this person is also pessimistic and sarcastic. A pointed tip combined with a broad nose indicates astuteness and materialistic tendencies.

Straight nose

This indicates loyalty, balanced judgement and self-sacrifice. It also expresses a strong need for affection which is not always easy to fulfil, as the subject seeks absolute love.

Crooked or asymmetrical nose

The oblique line of the nose indicates inner conflict not due to external trauma. It also reveals a superior sensibility which seeks its own truth over and above convention and conformity.

Upturned nose

A happy and optimistic nature which cannot stand complications and throws itself lightheartedly into everything that excites the subject's thirst for life is indicated by this nose. These people have the ability to give themselves totally to their loved ones, demanding in return as much dedication and respect. Of a touchy nature, people with upturned noses are capable of reacting violently if offended or betrayed. Luckily, they rarely bear a grudge.

Snub nose

This is characteristic of docile, simple people, who tend to go along with other people's wishes. If the nose is soft as well, the subject is prone to complaining about everything and seeks protective love. These types can be very appealing, however, for they possess a childlike vulnerability. Snub-nosed women fare better than men for this reason.

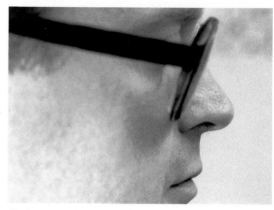

Fairly short, straight noses like this indicate good judgement, plus a strong need for affection

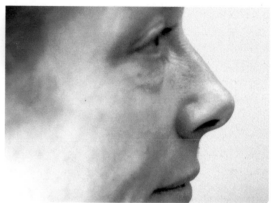

A large, rounded nose characterizes a cautious, artistic and honest person

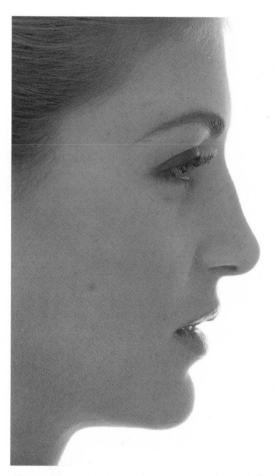

The small bump in this nose shows someone who works hard, while a rounded tip reveals enjoyment of life

This prominent, curved nose denotes stubbornness and a talent for making money

Faintly tilted, short noses like this reveal imagination and a degree of optimism

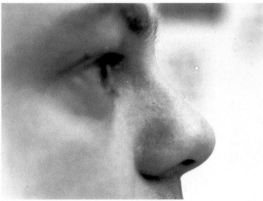

A gentle snub tip to this nose shows a desire to please and a childish sense of humour

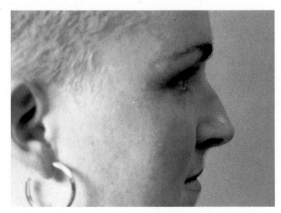

Aquiline noses signal creativity, leadership qualities and a dominant personality

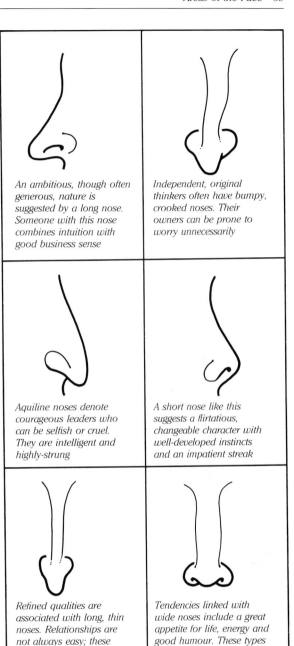

An ambitious, though often generous, nature is suggested by a long nose. Someone with this nose combines intuition with good business sense

Independent, original thinkers often have bumpy, crooked noses. Their owners can be prone to worry unnecessarily

Aquiline noses denote courageous leaders who can be selfish or cruel. They are intelligent and highly-strung

A short nose like this suggests a flirtatious, changeable character with well-developed instincts and an impatient streak

Refined qualities are associated with long, thin noses. Relationships are not always easy; these people can be moody

Tendencies linked with wide noses include a great appetite for life, energy and good humour. These types enjoy spending money

In a dream about noses the shape of the nose determines the meaning of the dream: a bulbous nose reflects good personal relationships, and a red one foretells the loss of something important. A long nose in a dream denotes impulsive actions whereas a turned-up one means promises will not be kept.

The ears

The size and shape of the ears reveal character tendencies more than any other part of the face. In ancient times, the shape of the lobes was considered particularly significant.

The ear is one of the most distinguishing features of the face. Unlike other features, it does not change shape as the face develops, it only changes in size. Reading people's characters from their ears is a very old science. In ancient Rome, people with big ears and fleshy lobes were considered balanced people with generous natures. On the other hand, those who had small ears with pale lobes were regarded as dangerous in some way. Caesar, as well as being wary of thin people, guarded against having people with small ears around him. Napoleon was advised to expel a captain from his bodyguard because he was endowed with 'ears as tiny as his mind and pale as his fidelity'. In the eighteenth century, the shape of the ear was said to indicate a talent for music. Modern physiognomy, too, takes the size and shape of the ear into account in judging whether or not a person is musical. Another curious example concerns the American Indians who still consider people with particularly well-developed ears as able to hear the voice of the deified spirit, Manitu.

High ears
If the top of the ear comes higher than the eyebrow line, you are dealing with a simple character who is endowed with remarkable common sense and an instinctual nature.

Low ears
Ears a little lower than normal, level with the base of the nose, indicate unusual intelligence and a lively mind.

Flap-ears
Sticking-out ears are typical of very brave, proud people who tend to be slightly aggressive physically or psychologically. These are the ears of a person who is always seeking new sensations and imagines great adventures.

Very flat ears
Very flat ears belong to shy people. These people are often inconstant and sometimes egocentric.

Big ears
Larger than average ears (more than 65 mm long and 36 mm wide) reveal an expansive, sensual and sometimes intrusive nature.

Small ears
A very small ear is typical of people who are sensitive, thoughtful and rather introverted. They find it quite difficult to communicate with others, but when they establish a friendship, it lasts a long time.

Ears with rounded edges
This ear indicates common sense, vitality and a tendency towards intellectual activity.

Thin or non-existent edges
These are the sign of an extrovert, restless character which tends to act on impulse, sometimes in an aggressive way.

Attached lobe
A lobe which is entirely attached to the ear denotes an impulsive and often angry nature, and repressed instincts.

Fleshy lobe
A full, fleshy pink lobe is a sign of a lively, sensual and witty character. It also indicates jealousy.

Soft, delicate lobe
This belongs to a person with a refined mind, who sometimes lacks vitality. This person tends to romanticize,

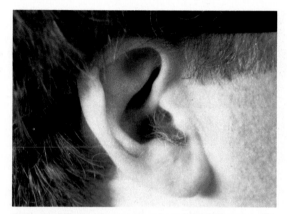

Fleshy, medium-sized ears with a deep cavity indicate a well-balanced communicator who has wide-ranging interests

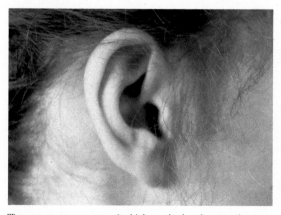

These neat ears are set quite high up the head, suggesting intelligence and sensitivity

and he or she seeks a gentle, loving relationship. He or she also tends to isolate himself or herself from others and, in some cases, may have to overcome sexual inhibitions.

Cold ears

An ear which is always cold and pale reveals a nervous temperament prone to anxiety.

Faun's ears

A narrow, forward-pointing ear denotes astuteness, maliciousness and intrigue. The subject seeks amorous adventures and secret love affairs.

Musical ears

A very wide conch (the cavity leading to the auditory canal) denotes a gift for music. This is even more pronounced if the inner ear is very large, the edge is well shaped and the lobe nicely detached from the face. The subject seeks harmony in life and in relationships.

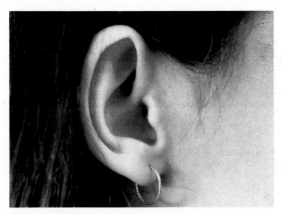

Here, slender rectangular ears denote intellectual ability and restlessness. Nervous exhaustion could affect her health

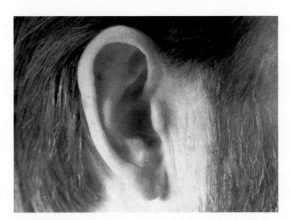

Long ears with small lobes reveal a kind, intuitive person who has self-control plus curiosity about life

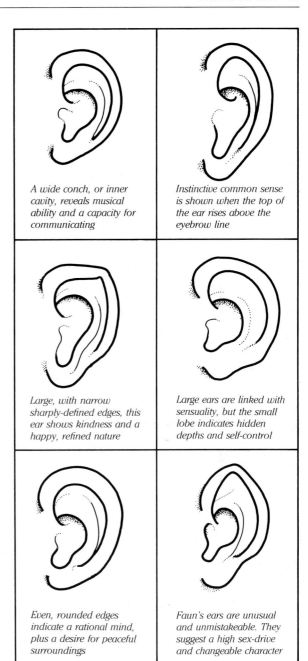

A wide conch, or inner cavity, reveals musical ability and a capacity for communicating

Instinctive common sense is shown when the top of the ear rises above the eyebrow line

Large, with narrow sharply-defined edges, this ear shows kindness and a happy, refined nature

Large ears are linked with sensuality, but the small lobe indicates hidden depths and self-control

Even, rounded edges indicate a rational mind, plus a desire for peaceful surroundings

Faun's ears are unusual and unmistakeable. They suggest a high sex-drive and changeable character

Red ears

Ears which are noticeably red all the time indicate an uncertain temper and touchy personality. This person is very thin skinned, and possibly suffers from high blood-pressure. Occasional flushing denotes embarrassment, physical attraction, or repressed anger.

The mouth

Together with the eyes, the mouth conveys personality most immediately, betraying sympathetic or antipathetic vibrations, coldness or warmth. But in order to read the meaning in a mouth, the lips must also be classified.

The mouth is another of the first elements from which people form an opinion of a person standing before them. It is a significant form of expression and, apart from the eyes, people remember actors' and actresses' mouths more than any other facial feature. In a physiognomy survey, forty out of a hundred women recalled best the *eyes* of a man whose characteristics they were asked to memorize. Sixty out of a hundred women remembered best his mouth.

In 1956, in the United States, a major producer of low alcohol drinks was looking for a masculine image for advertising. The type had to be 'young, strong and healthy looking', and, above all, have a pleasing mouth. This was because in various shots for the advertising campaign, he had to appear in the act of raising a glass to his lips.

A survey was carried out among women by an advertising agency launching a Californian rosé wine. The campaign was aimed at women, the slogan being, 'She likes it, too'. The majority of respondents favoured Gregory Peck's mouth. Physiognomy scholars describe this mouth type as half-closed. The survey confirmed Gregory Peck's popularity among women, and film producers began looking for 'Gregory Peck mouths' among actors. Although this incident may sound frivolous, it is very revealing. According to the unanimous opinion of a number of men in a survey, the most sensual women's mouths are well-defined with full lips; whereas women find men's mouths sexy not because of the shape and type of lips, but because of their expression. The 'Gregory Peck' mouth, or the half-closed mouth, is a sign of a dynamic, generous personality, a sharp mind and of someone who finds it easy to relate to others. These are the kind of characteristics which women generally look for in their partners.

More than any other characteristic, sensuality is expressed by the mouth. If you know how to read it, the mouth can tell you how committed a person is to love and sex – according to the mouth's shape, size and expression.

Large mouth
When the mouth is big and wide with full lips, it is a sign of an exuberant, sensual nature which eagerly seeks new experiences and emotions.

Small mouth
This reveals a lack of energy and nearly always belongs to people with modest ambitions who operate within a limited sphere. Sometimes, however, beneath this humble

Full, fleshy lips like these (above and left) are a certain sign of a passionate, romantic personality

When a mouth has naturally upturned corners it is attractive, and shows an extrovert character

Upturned lips, especially if they are often parted, denote a good-humoured, optimistic extrovert

Perfect, heart-shaped lips can be very seductive and are a sign of success with the opposite sex

Thin lips typically belong to logical, self-controlled individuals who are careful with money

A pouting, down-turned mouth denotes a wilful, stubborn character who is often hard to please

A straight, thin upper lip denotes far-sightedness, business acumen, and meanness with money

Half-open mouths are linked with frank, trusting personalities whose naivety may create difficulties

Protruding upper lips often accompany slightly buck teeth, indicating shyness and a childlike personality

Well-defined protruding lower lips are associated with jealous, possessive, egotistical characteristics

façade, the subject conceals great aspirations which have been repressed but which could at any moment come to the fore.

Open mouth

People whose mouths are often open, even as adults, express a childlike candour or uncertainty. They are easily-influenced people who are looking for rôle models, and who leave decision-making to others.

Half-open mouth

An affectionate, sociable and dynamic nature is revealed by this mouth. This person has a keen, open mind and his or her relations with others are always characterized by generosity and understanding.

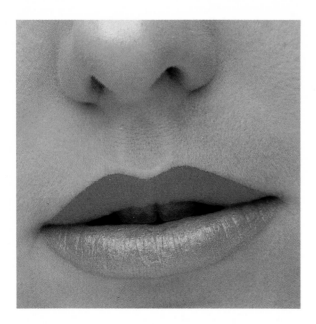

A pretty Cupid's bow suggests great femininity

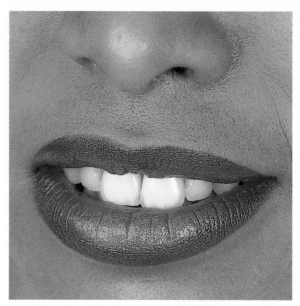

Great vitality is attributed to those with full lips

Closed mouth

When the mouth is always closed, the lips tight and the corners turned down, it is a sign of a gloomy, pessimistic nature, prone to seeing only the negative side of life. People with this type of mouth feel as though they are victims of circumstance and have little ability to change the direction of their lives.

Laughing mouth

The smiling mouth with full lips and the corners turned upwards belongs to an optimist who sees the positive side of things. He or she enjoys good food and the pleasures of family life and love.

Full lips

An affectionate and vital nature which is sometimes passionate is revealed by full lips. They also indicate goodness of heart and an ability to sympathize and share others' feelings. If the lips protrude, it is a sign that sometimes this person lies, but usually only to make themselves more appealing to others.

Thin lips

These are typical of people who are good at controlling their own emotions and thoughts. Often, these subjects are accused of lack of interest, but in most cases they simply need to withdraw in order to concentrate. Only if the thin lips are accompanied by dull eyes do they indicate falseness and a calculating nature.

Wide lips

Very wide lips (more than 55 mm in men and 47 mm in women) denote sensuality and the desire for happiness and possession. They are a sign of vitality and jealousy.

Small lips

If the lips are less than 50 mm wide in a man or 40 mm wide in a woman, it is a sign that the head rules the heart, but not exclusively. At times, these people can be flirtatious. Small lips denote fragile health.

Heart-shaped lips

These are a sign of an interesting person who lives life to the full. In a man, they can reveal an effeminate nature. In either sex, if the lips are very full in the centre, this denotes sensuality.

Protruding upper lip

This is typical of kind-hearted, sensitive people who withdraw from aggression and violence. Sometimes it signals lack of energy.

Barely visible upper lip

If the upper lip is so thin that it can barely be seen and is also straight, it shows a calculating, rational character. In intellectuals, it sometimes denotes refined creative and artistic talents.

Overhanging lower lip

A very protruding, full lower lip is a sign of a jealous, sensual, authoritarian and greedy character.

Downturned lips

If the corners of the mouth are turned down, they reveal a sceptical, proud character. This person is in continual conflict with himself or herself.

Upturned lips

If the corners of the mouth are turned upwards, it is a sign of a jovial, witty character who can be presumptuous, but is also endearing.

The chin

The lower part of the face governs the instincts, the subject's degree of willpower and combative spirit. This is inferred by the everyday expression that someone has a weak or strong chin.

The chin and jaw together make up the lower part of the face, which physiognomy associates with instinctive and organic life. To establish the degree of willpower a person has, measure the distance between the top of the forehead and the tip of the chin, and the distance from the start of the nose to the tip of the chin. If the latter measurement is more than a third of the first, this indicates that willpower is a dominant characteristic.

Broad chin
A wide, square chin reveals an ambitious, strong-willed and sometimes selfish character. If a wide chin is accompanied by a wide jaw, it means that the subject also has physical stamina. If the chin is so large that it is discordant with the rest of the face, it indicates despotism.

Narrow chin
A delicate, sensitive, hesitant nature which rarely takes the initiative belongs to this person. If a narrow chin is accompanied by a wide forehead, it is a sign of an acute mind and artistic talent.

Round chin
This is a typical feature of people with great initiative, who enjoy new experiences and sensations. They are also very intuitive. In their relations with others, these subjects are affable and generous, conciliatory and kind. A round chin can sometimes also be a sign of inner dissatisfaction and a longing for material pleasures.

Long chin
A long chin generally shows energy, firmness and organizational ability. If the chin is particularly thin and bony, it also denotes enterprise, common sense and love of order. If it is very pointed, it means the subject has a nervous and dissipated nature.

A fleshy, protruding chin reveals a powerful, materialistic nature. Here, ambition combines with kindness and humour

Three different chins: classical (far left), dominant (centre), and slightly receding (right), drawn by Leonardo da Vinci

Long, pointed chin
A tendency to give orders and impose their authority belongs to these people. They have an ambitious nature and, to achieve their aims, they are prepared to give low priority to their feelings. This is particularly true of people with a long nose as well.

Slightly pointed chin
A slightly pointed chin belongs to people who are ambitious but lack the courage and optimism needed to throw themselves into business ventures.

A firm chin shows strength of character

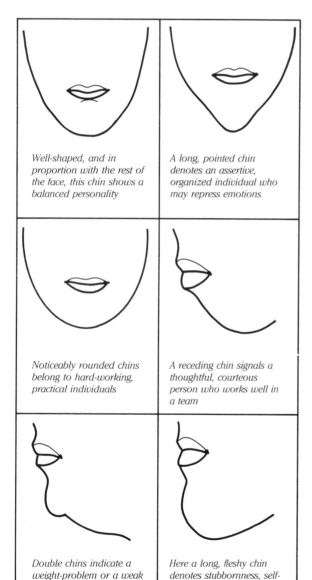

Well-shaped, and in proportion with the rest of the face, this chin shows a balanced personality

A long, pointed chin denotes an assertive, organized individual who may repress emotions

Noticeably rounded chins belong to hard-working, practical individuals

A receding chin signals a thoughtful, courteous person who works well in a team

Double chins indicate a weight-problem or a weak jawline

Here a long, fleshy chin denotes stubbornness, self-confidence and a powerful personality

Small, well-shaped chin
When a small chin is in perfect harmony with the rest of the face, it indicates remarkable inner strength. Economic success does not matter to these people, but their love life and spiritual life does. They rise above problems because they are adaptable and sensible.

Receding chin
These people have fluctuating physical energy. Their willpower, constancy and decisiveness are weakened when their energy is at a low ebb. They often compensate for it with kindness and gentleness. They can be diffident when they want to defend themselves against criticism.

Dimpled chin
Dimples are usually thought to signal a sympathetic and seductive character. In fact their meaning depends on the structure of the chin. In a wide, square chin a dimple reinforces qualities of willpower and energy. In a receding chin it is a sign of inconstancy and insecurity.

Very small chin
This reveals the dreamy and imaginative nature of someone who lives in an unreal world.

Fat, fleshy chin
This denotes physical energy, a high sex drive, decisiveness and self-confidence.

Double chin
Sometimes this is linked to health problems. When it is not, it denotes a rather lazy, apathetic character who is content to fulfil his or her material needs, renouncing other commitments and responsibilities.

How to analyse a face

Having acquired a basic knowledge of physiognomy, you are well equipped to analyse the basic character of those around you. To start with, look at this photograph of Sophia Loren.

A wide forehead with a clearly defined hairline and strong eyebrows (thinned by the beautician's tweezers but originally thick) indicate a quick mind. The eyes are large and liquid, signalling a generous, sometimes introverted, nature. The subject has a tendency to remember the difficult times she has had; she acts in the light of past experience, but does not manage to free herself from all the fears that beset her.

Sophia Loren's nose, well proportioned and strong, is a sign that she is open to new ideas. Her mouth is large and well defined, which indicates a willingness to communicate with others, although she keeps to a small circle of friends that she knows. Her attitude to strangers is underlined by the way in which she holds her cigarette pointing towards the person she is speaking to, almost as if to keep them at a distance, indicating that she remains on the defensive.

Her large hands and strong wrists show constancy and an ability to take on stressful commitments.

On the whole, the subject belongs to the category of people destined for success but capable of only partially enjoying the benefits this brings. Insecurity is a very common characteristic among people who succeed in show business.

3

The Head, Face and Body

Both physiognomists and phrenologists pay attention to the size and shape of the whole head. Complaining that somebody is big-headed is a common figure of speech. Experts have identified many kinds of head shape which, like the face itself, can reveal useful clues to character.

Many more ancient ideas about personality, as revealed by the size and shape of the head, are still part of everyday speech. Throughout literature are references to large, noble heads, strong or weak profiles and so on. It is an insult to call someone 'a pin-head' – meaning that they lack brains. In fact, a small head does not necessarily house a feeble mind, but may equally indicate someone who works better in a team and has no wish to dominate others. The word 'head' is used to mean boss, or person in charge, while to give a profile of someone means to give a brief biography, which is exactly what you will get by studying a face sideways on.

Large heads, especially when they are slightly out of proportion with the rest of the body, may also remind us of babies and small children. Babies' heads are naturally like this, and are usually very rounded with domed foreheads. Some psychologists and anthropologists have conducted research which suggests that women are particularly attracted to domed foreheads, because they are answering to an innate call to love and care for their babies.

It is also worthwhile looking at how someone holds their head. An upright, relaxed posture always suggests confidence – but if the head droops then it is a sure sign either of depression or of someone lost in thought. By checking other facial features and the general appearance as well, you will soon be able to determine subtle differences.

The size of the head

If every feature is significant, the head as a whole is even more so. A careful study of the head provides the key to personality.

A human head has a circumference, measured above the ears, of between about 54 and 60 cm for men and 53 and 57 cm for' women. Heads may be even bigger or smaller in circumference but, if they are in proportion with the body, should still be considered normal. The size and shape of the head both face on and in profile should be examined.

Large head
If the head is bigger than average, it generally shows intellectual and reasoning abilities. These people rarely lack confidence and are usually successful in life.

Over-large head
In this case, it seems justified to call someone a big-head! An over-large head is a sign of stubbornness and inflexibility. It can sometimes indicate glandular problems.

Small head
A small head denotes a alert mind, changeable moods, thoughtlessness and impulsiveness.

Too small a head
This is often a sign of a passive character, weak and easily influenced. It is as if the personality has never fully developed; although these people may be reasonably intelligent they lack drive.

Very wide head between the ears
This person is practical and has a good head for business. Spiritual qualities may be lacking, however.

Very wide, convex head
When the whole of the top of the head (seen from the front) is very wide, it means that this person has great spiritual aspirations which make them live in a poetical dreamworld, confusing fantasy with reality.

Less wide, less convex head
Less width at the top and side of the skull are a sign of a decidedly realistic person who has his or her feet on the ground and hates sentimentality, romance and idealism.

Almost pointed head
A head which is very wide over the ears (more than 16 cm wide from one ear to the other) and is almost pointed at the crown is typical of an aggressive, authoritarian person. He or she will probably be jealous, possessive, greedy and obsessed with material possessions.

Oval head
When the head is very elongated and rounded over the skull (egg-shaped), it is a sign of lofty thoughts, a religious spirit and the need to be totally devoted to a great ideal. The old slang term 'egg head' stems from the typical

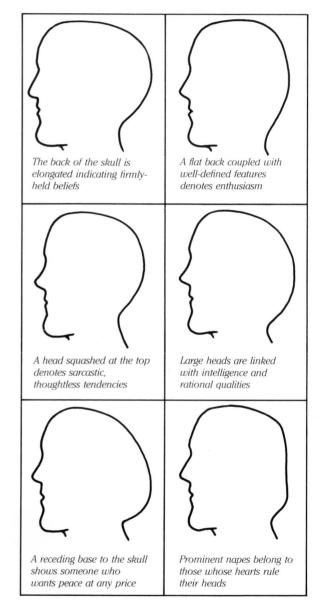

The back of the skull is elongated indicating firmly-held beliefs

A flat back coupled with well-defined features denotes enthusiasm

A head squashed at the top denotes sarcastic, thoughtless tendencies

Large heads are linked with intelligence and rational qualities

A receding base to the skull shows someone who wants peace at any price

Prominent napes belong to those whose hearts rule their heads

characteristics of oval-headed people.

Regular head
This conforms to the average size, is in proportion with the body and at the same time widens a little at the top. It belongs to well-balanced people with alert minds who are both mentally and physically fit.

Sylvester Stallone's head is remarkably wide between the ears, revealing good business sense and a pronounced stubborn streak. His exceptionally thick neck bears witness to hours of weight-training

Wide at the front, flat at the back

This is a head which is nearly as broad from side to side as it is from front to back (brachycephalous). It belongs to energetic, impulsive people who throw themselves into things and do not beat about the bush.

Head squashed at the top

When seen in profile, if the top of the head seems flat it means that subjects have a very crude view of reality. They tend to be brusque and can be fiercely sarcastic.

Very prominent, convex back of the head

This characteristic is often found in tenacious, faithful people who are unshakeable in their convictions and beliefs.

Receding head at the back

When the dome of the skull slants downwards from front to back, it denotes someone who has given up struggling in life and accepts compromises and humiliation – anything for a quiet life.

Very prominent nape

This is a sign of a character which is largely ruled by emotion. If the lower part of the nape is also prominent, it means that this person is also very sensual and passionate.

The perfectly balanced, even shape of this woman's head suggests a well-adjusted personality

The face in profile

The profile sums up the face, as caricaturists are well aware when they wish to capture a subject's personality. The most prominent features of a face are emphasized in profile, so important deductions about a subject's character and psyche can be made by a study of it. A profile may be described as being predominantly concave, vertical, convex, mixed or normal.

Concave profile
This is when the base of the forehead curves inwards and the area from the nose to the chin is concave. Such a profile reveals a rather cold character endowed with remarkable self-control. His or her behaviour is usually contradictory and uncertain, often relying unnecessarily on the judgement of others. This profile is also, however, a sign of many talents; it shows prudence, reflection, fidelity, intelligence and sensibility.

Vertical profile
Profiles which have few protrusions or hollows are called vertical or flat. This type of profile denotes a sober nature and acute powers of observation and judgement. People with this profile have the ability to learn fast and to analyse and process all they observe. They have strong characters, are realistic, do not allow themselves to be influenced easily and tend to be obstinate in their ideas and opinions.

Convex profile
Convex refers to profiles with a very prominent forehead, a pointed nose, prominent lips and a receding chin. This profile is found in people who have very agile minds, who think and act with remarkable speed and have a healthy curiosity. They also have the desire to realize many different projects at once. In practice, these individuals may not meet the demands of their enthusiasm; however, they are always able to recharge themselves with new ideas, and they find ways of achieving positive results, in both economic and professional spheres.

Mixed profile
This is one in which convexity and concavity alternate in a curious fashion (see picture, opposite). It belongs to people who have a strong, contradictory and sometimes unpredictable character. They may be geniuses or artists. Such a profile can also indicate a tendency to flout every moral rule with anarchic instinct. It is always a sign of an original personality.

A regular profile
When the profile is harmonious and the three principle parts (forehead, nose and chin) well proportioned, the subject has a balanced, pleasant character. He or she will not be very imaginative or creative but will always fit into family, social and professional environments.

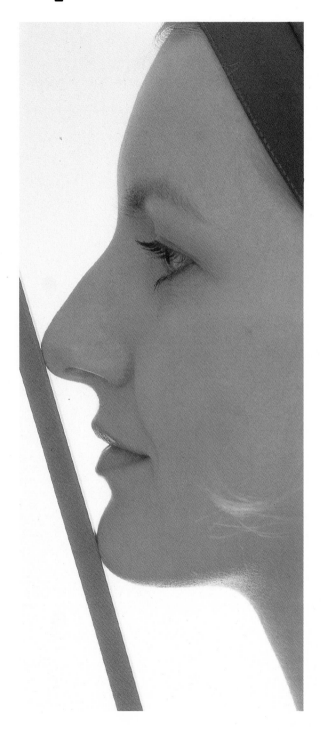

The left and right sides of the face

The left and right sides of the face always differ – sometimes strikingly. Each side reveals different aspects of your personality. If you cover up one side of your face with a sheet of paper, or take two identical photos of your face and mask out the left side on one photograph and the right side on the other, the differences between the two sides will become more obvious.

The left side

The left side of the face, or the heart side, reveals the instinctive and hereditary aspects of your personality. This very ancient theory has been confirmed by modern science through the studies of psychologists from the University of Pennsylvania. They examined thousands of faces and concluded: 'When we undergo stress that produces fear, anger, anguish, aversion (and also when we experience intense joy), we set in motion the muscles of the left side of the face with the greatest force. The right hand side remains much more controlled, sometimes almost impassive.'

Thus the left hand side of the face, if examined closely, more than the right hand side reflects adversities and general well-being. Small or large wrinkles which mark this side are signs of traumas and passions we have experienced in life. The Indian saddhus teach: 'Stand in front of a mirror and command your brain to control the emotions. That way the left hand side of your face will remain younger and smoother.'

The right side

This is the side that reflects the amount of intelligence and self-control a person has – all that he or she has acquired by way of experience and psychological maturity. This side

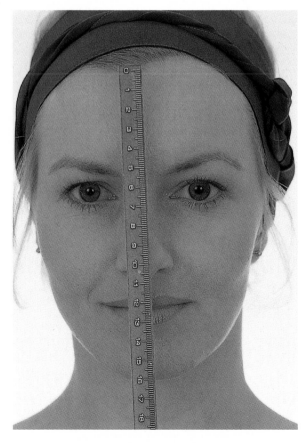

of the face, because it does not reflect emotion to the same extent, is more relaxed. It is the façade that we unconsciously want to show others. Film and television stars frequently prefer to have the right side of their faces photographed: this side is smoother, livelier and more expressive than the left side.

Self presentation

If you are going on a first date or to a meeting, why not show the right side of your face more than the left? Your best side is more attractive and animated, creating a better impression. But if you want to be known and loved for your faults, then show your real profile – the left one.

In this detail from Breakfast, *by Paul Signac, the artist has deliberately exaggerated masculine and feminine traits in the profiles*

The shape of the body

What makes you the shape you are? Most people know a little about genetic inheritance – and whenever a new child enters the family everyone enjoys trying to see who it takes after. In these health-conscious days, we are aware of the importance of a well-balanced diet and the effects of poor nutrition or over-eating, but did you also realize that your body shapes itself in response to your personality?

A number of researchers, including F.M. Alexander, founder of the Alexander technique, Ida Rolf and Dr Ken Dychtwald, have contributed to this field of discovery. They maintain that the human body is shaped by habitual thought patterns and emotional upsets. In addition, children tend to copy the postures and movements of their parents, so if your father or mother slouches it is more than likely that you will follow suit.

Character clues must be taken in the context of family background, job, sports, hobbies, illness and injury, which can all change both body shape and posture as well. Physiognomy, too, states that by studying the body you can gain valuable insights into character.

Large, Medium and Small

Shakespeare's Julius Caesar surrounded himself with fat people, believing them to be more trustworthy than thin ones. Centuries later, most people still equate well-covered endomorphs – as they are scientifically classified – with warm-hearted, non-aggressive personality traits. Fat people are supposed to be jolly, safe and cuddly, rather like lovable teddy-bears.

Although many fat people have slow metabolisms and tend to be placid, they may also be very insecure and feel unattractive. This was not always the case. In the past, being overweight was a sign of wealth, for poor people could not afford the quantities of food it takes to achieve an expansive figure.

Ectomorph is the name given to very skinny people, whose fashionable heyday was during the 1960s when top models like Twiggy were supposed to be ideal women. Thin, bony people are usually thought of as tense, quiet, and intelligent. They have a lot of nervous energy, burning up food faster than most, although they generally eat a normal amount.

This is one of the most obvious differences between a genuine ectomorph and an anorexic. Anorexia nervosa is an eating disorder mainly affecting young women, and results in lethargy, depression, and a totally false self-image. Bona fide ectomorphs are rarely lethargic.

A slender, well-exercised body combining both ecto- and mesomorph characteristics

The third major category to look for is the mesomorph. They are naturally muscular, medium-sized people with a tendency to gain weight as they grow older. Mesomorphs are independent, adventurous types who need regular exercise and can sometimes be slightly lazy. The recent fitness boom has done wonders for their image; muscular bodies are now the height of fashion and even the models in magazines have gained a few curves.

Having identified these basic shapes, you are ready to look for what are called 'body splits'. These, experts believe, are created by a mysterious combination of personality and circumstance – and can be consciously changed through certain kinds of massage, exercise, and mental effort.

Top to Bottom

To identify this category you must view the body in two sections, divided by the waist. The upper half of the body represents the extrovert part of the personality: by using our arms we express love and affection; we greet other people; we strike them in anger and are generally active. Our lower half is less demonstrative. This part supports the rest of the body; digests food and is associated with love-making and child-bearing. So our introvert lower half is strongly associated with earthy feelings – home, children, food and stability.

Two very obvious examples of this split are a broad-hipped woman with a relatively small bosom; or a man whose barrel-like chest and powerful arms are supported by noticeably thinner legs and narrow hips. The woman described will be emotional and feminine, and her home, family and friends will be very important to her. She is likely to be reserved, loyal and practical, preferring a routine and organized life-style.

The man with a large chest and thinner legs will display a very different personality. He will be active and outwardly confident, but will have trouble expressing his emotions and find it difficult to be reflective. As you gain experience, you should be able to spot more subtle examples by looking for the following clues:

- Weight distribution

- Muscular development

- Grace and co-ordination – which half of the body moves more fluidly?

- Health (apply this to yourself, or people close to you). Does one half of the body seem healthier or more relaxed? Look for tense shoulders or stiff legs and hips.

Overweight people, like this endomorph, seldom feel secure or attractive

Back to Front

You rarely see your own back except when trying on clothes, or perhaps in a photograph. So although you could easily recognize a friend from behind, what your own back view looks like may come as a bit of a shock.

The front of the body is associated with the self. When you look in the mirror, you face the world with this image firmly in mind. Meanwhile, the back – hidden from sight – represents your private, unconscious self. Just as you do in your subconscious, you tend to store suppressed rage and fear in your back.

If you are someone who puts their back into life but does nothing to relieve stress and tension, then your back is guaranteed to be a lot more tense than your front. Anyone who has trouble being assertive without losing their temper is also likely to have some kind of back trouble. Constantly suppressed anger is usually stored in the back, for when you feel like fighting but do not, you automatically stiffen the spine to support the vulnerable front of the body. When this becomes permanent, you have literally put everything behind you – and back pain is the result.

Look around you, and you will soon see that every back tells a story, whether a back which is bowed down by heavy burdens, a stiff and rigid back revealing inhibitions, or a straight, graceful spine capable of dealing with everything life has to offer. What kind of back belongs to you?

Torso and Limbs

Finally, there is the split between the torso and the limbs. The torso represents your centre, while your arms and legs extend out into the world. You use your limbs to move and express yourself in both work and play, but the torso is usually hidden away by clothes and only revealed to other people under special circumstances – such as at the beach, or when making love. It symbolizes your private world, the introvert part of your personality.

Arms and legs, however, are much more public. Generally speaking, extrovert people use their arms much more dramatically than shyer personalities. Active, energetic people often restlessly tap their feet and shift their position a lot during conversation – for they are impatient, and long to be getting on with their next project. Characters in this category often have well-developed limbs because they are usually fond of some kind of sport.

Withdrawn, thoughtful types are more inhibited. They tend to bottle up their emotions and have trouble saying what they want to say. This type may have weak, poorly-developed arms and legs extending from a relatively solid body – as if they were frightened to reach out to others, or stray very far from home. Introverts do not make theatrical gestures with their arms, are typically more interested in ideas and feelings than in activity and may use up considerable physical energy in mental concentration.

Laurel and Hardy clearly demonstrate two completely contrasting body types: slim, nervous Laurel and fat, sensible Hardy

The head in relation to the body

Some people are almost totally unaware of their bodies. They tend to dislike, or avoid, exercise; their eating habits are often unbalanced, too, for they have become uncertain about when – and how much – to eat.

Today's sedentary life-styles have contributed to this trend. Few adults in Western society know what their bodies are saying until it is too late. Hopefully, health and fitness trends will reverse the process and add another dimension to everyday life.

Those who do not think of their bodies are usually intelligent, often highly trained, and tend to ignore their feelings. The head, they argue, is the seat of intellect, and feelings stem from the body. Such characters value logic and reason above sensations and emotional reactions, and prefer to ignore their bodies, which are likely to be flabby, even when slim. Since the head is part of the body, its position in relation to the body can clearly reveal both mental and emotional traits.

Lowered head
This belongs to a submissive, possibly depressed person who cannot face life and has trouble communicating.

Protruding head
This person sticks his or her neck out and thrusts the head forward. He or she is anxious, forward-looking and tends to worry about things unnecessarily.

Protruding jaw
When the jaw, as well as the head, noticeably protrudes, you are dealing with an obstinate, determined type who will fight for what he or she believes to be right.

Upright, rigid head
A rigidly upright head signals someone who is under a lot of stress and feels that he or she must control everything. Such people will rarely admit that they are unable to cope, but struggle on regardless. They are highly responsible, ambitious and frequently suffer from an aching neck and shoulders.

Receding jawline
A receding jawline occurs when the head is pulled back, so that the chin is tucked in towards the neck. This person is, on the whole, afraid of life and finds it difficult to speak up for themselves. Do not automatically associate this type of chin with an inherited weak chin. Jawlines are moveable, and affected by characteristic postures.

This girl's nicely-proportioned body supports a well-balanced head – suggesting she enjoys both mental and physical equilibrium

4

Details of the Head and Neck

Having mastered the basic skills of phrenology you can turn your attention to finer details of the face, head and neck such as the eyebrows, wrinkles, and even the tongue.

Hair, or the lack of it, teeth and eyebrows are quite easy to alter cosmetically. But if you are in any doubt about how much of a person is as nature intended, you can still learn how to read their smile – and take a good look at the neck.

The neck reveals your approximate age and some glandular disturbances and acts as a symbolic channel between the brain and the body. If someone is very stressed, their neck is usually one of the first places to register tension. The expression, 'It's a pain in the neck' is used by people when they find a task difficult to perform. Always combine your analysis of the shape of the neck with a few observations about how it is being used. Ideally, the neck should be flexible, relaxed, and reasonably upright – just like the rest of the body.

It is often said that in old age we get the face we deserve. Although skin-type, exposure to sunlight and diet are inextricably linked with the ageing process, it is not how *many* wrinkles a person has, but what *kind* of wrinkles. A better name for wrinkles would be expression lines – and that is just what they are.

Some experts have suggested that anyone who displays noticeable lines before the age of thirty is easily influenced, moody, and often exceptionally sensitive. Calmer natures acquire wrinkles later in life, because they do not react to events so obviously. Similarly, people who keep things to themselves will take longer to show lines simply because their faces are less mobile.

The smile

People have always been fascinated by smiles, for human beings are the only creatures on earth who can, and do, show pleasure in this way. Smiles not only reveal your current mood and basic personality, but also affect everyone who sees them.

Some in-depth research conducted in California by Professor Paul Ekman has come up with evidence to suggest that smiles are catching. When you are smiling, it seems, the whole world is inclined to smile with you because human beings are emotionally affected by the facial expressions of others. This pioneering research claims that if you are frequently faced with miserable people, you will eventually start feeling low yourself. By smiling yourself and seeing other smiling faces, your mood is very likely to improve.

Old teachings on the art of physiognomy all pay great attention to the mouth, believing it to be one of the most telling indicators of character there is. They always suggest that students look both at the shape of the mouth and the smile. Research has isolated three broad smile categories, each expressing different emotions and using different muscles.

Genuine, heart-felt smiles signal joy and happiness. Ekman and his team called them 'felt smiles' – which is exactly what they are. In real life they light up faces of all ages, but can be difficult to recognize in photographs unless you look closely – especially at the eyes. For a real smile uses two distinct sets of muscles – the *zygomatic major*, which raise the corners of the lips, and the *orbicularis oculi*, which lift up the cheeks and draw the skin around the eye-socket inwards.

Overwhelming emotions cause these muscles to react like this, and the deeper the feeling the more noticeable the result on the face. Another clue to watch for is the

Princess Diana's charming smile just reveals her upper teeth, confirming rumours of her innate shyness

The mysterious half-smile of the Mona Lisa is especially noticeable in her eyes, which convey warmth and wry amusement

actual length of the smile – scientists have observed that really happy smiles last for a maximum of four seconds.

Genuine smiles

There are three main kinds of happy smile, but never base any analysis on the mouth alone. Unless there is that give-away crinkle around the eyes, you are not observing a genuine smile.

Closed mouth, or simple smile

This smile belongs to someone who is probably enjoying a private joke, or perhaps remembering past pleasures. Above all, smiling to yourself is an activity you do not always share with others – and indeed you could easily be alone when you smile like this. The most famous example belongs to the enigmatic Mona Lisa, whose secret smile has puzzled art-lovers for centuries.

Upper teeth smile

Most often seen when friends say hello, this smile reveals the upper teeth only. If this is the habitual smile of someone you know, they may be a bit reserved or shy. Many years ago, this was considered the only kind of smile you could display in polite society – exposing your lower teeth to public gaze was thought to be very vulgar.

Broad, open smile

Here both sets of teeth are seen, while the mouth stretches

wide and opens slightly. Broad smiles belong to good-natured, exuberant personalities who love life and often find it very funny. Dazzling grins like this can easily grow larger and larger until they turn into a full-bodied laugh.

False smiles

False smiles fill newspapers, magazines and very often wedding photographs. They do not always mean someone is untrustworthy, but can point to a situation where smiling is obligatory. Actors, salesmen, airline personnel and others who are encouraged to be charming and cheerful at

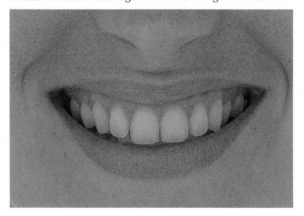

work may not always be able to summon up emotions to match their expressions – so they fake them. Here are the clues which will turn you into an expert smile-detector:

● Firstly, how do you feel? If somebody is trying to deceive you – for whatever reason – you will probably feel uncomfortable. You are certainly unlikely to say 'What a lovely smile', because subconsciously you already realize that it is not.

● Check the eyes, both for smile lines and warmth of expression. Even the most accomplished actors in the world cannot control their eyes or the muscles around them – so only the lips can lie.

● If the upper lip is raised in an exaggerated way, while the lower lip assumes a square shape and the jaw looks immobile – which it is, since the cheeks and eyes will not have been lifted up by real emotion – then the smile is a false one.

● An oblong smile with drawn-back lips showing both sets of teeth, in a poor imitation of a broad grin, is really a grimace. It can be spotted when someone is politely pretending to be pleased to see you, or amused by a tasteless joke.

● False smiles last longer than the real thing – and take longer to spread across the face. They are also more uneven. Watch for one side of the mouth rising fractionally higher than the other – giving an asymmetrical slant to the expression. Do not confuse this with the final type of smile, which is also asymmetrical.

● The miserable, or ironic, smile also signals a cover-up. Ironic smiles reveal an insecure and scornful nature. This smile belongs to an outwardly arrogant, inwardly uncertain person. Someone who normally smiles like this is also very self-protective; their smile is one of many barriers which they erect between themselves and the outside world.

● When you see a miserable smile, you are looking at someone who is putting on a brave face for the benefit of others. A lop-sided smile reveals resignation, defeat and inner unhappiness, as if half the mouth were smiling and the other half sunk in misery. This person has courage in the face of disaster, and believes very firmly that life must go on. He or she is usually a proud, private person who tends to suppress negative feelings, and so may suffer from a nervous disorder ranging from back-ache to a mysterious skin rash or upset stomach.

A genuine, happy smile signals a warm personality (above left), while a gum-revealing grin can be false and forced (left)

Laughter

Laughter, like smiles, has many subtle shades of meaning. You might politely titter when you are not really amused at all, snigger at a risqué joke, relax into a full-blooded belly laugh, or cackle hysterically from shock or surprise.

As with smiling, you have probably developed a characteristic and recognizable laugh which is as personal as your signature – although most people still laugh in slightly different ways depending upon the situation. Sadly, some people become so inhibited by the time they reach maturity they seldom laugh at all. Life, according to these characters, is no laughing matter – and if you know anyone like this you may be sure you are dealing with a repressed or depressed person.

So what is laughter? Expert opinion is divided on this question – partly because laughter serves a number of purposes. Threatening laughter of a kind has been observed in monkeys, and human beings sometimes laugh when they are feeling aggressive. This is why serious newspapers employ cartoonists, for by sending something up and making a frightening idea or situation seem comical, we are trying to overcome it. Similarly, sex is the butt of many jokes because it is such a sensitive subject. Humour makes it all seem less serious and embarrassing.

Pictures of laughing or crying people are sometimes hard to tell apart – and often laughter does lead to tears. 'I laughed till the tears ran down my face' is a common

Actress Joanna Lumley and her son illustrate the type of broad smile which can easily turn to laughter

enough saying. Many anthropologists believe the two reactions are closely linked, and certainly most people have laughed with relief once they have realized they are out of danger or no longer in a tense or difficult situation.

The best medicine

To many scientists, laughter is a serious business. Modern research has revealed that laughter not only uses fifteen different facial muscles, but positively affects every organ in the body. Breathing quickens as the laughing person inhales and exhales deeply through their vocal chords – exercising the face, neck, shoulders, stomach and diaphragm. Blood pressure tends to go down, and circulation improves as blood vessels close to the surface of the skin expand, sometimes visibly reddening the face. Oxygen levels in the blood increase, heart rate lowers, and the brain joins in by releasing natural pain-killing chemicals called beta-endorphins.

Such is the healing power of a good laugh that it has been dubbed 'stationary jogging', and credited by one French neurologist, Henri Rubinstein, with providing forty-five minutes of relaxation for every minute of laughter enjoyed. Many doctors in both Europe and America are now convinced that laughter plays an important role in healing and recovery from illness – while some go so far as to suggest that if we all laughed more often we might not fall ill at all.

Types of laugh

When using laughter analysis to help build up a picture of someone, remember to base your opinions on a range of observations. Some people find it hard to be themselves in the company of strangers – and several meetings could be necessary before you can be certain you have heard the kind of laughter which truly expresses their basic personality. Meanwhile, you can only assess their mood and whether they are introverts or extroverts. True extroverts, of course, have few inhibitions and are much easier to analyse straight away.

Bearing all this in mind, the following is a breakdown of the main kinds of laugh plus the predominant vowel sounds to listen for. The actual sound of the laugh is affected by the shape formed by the lips, and the amount of air inhaled and exhaled. Timid people tend to take more shallow breaths than bolder spirits, and so their laughter sounds thinner and lasts for a shorter time. Laughing is really very similar to singing – a good deep breath provides power and gives richness to the tone of voice.

An open-mouthed smile combines delight and surprise in this exuberant-looking example

A mouth making an 'e' shape; this person is unlikely to be expressing heartfelt amusement

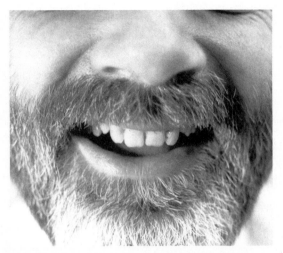

An open 'a' shaped mouth suggests a lively laugh and an open, vital personality

Guffaw

If it is frequent, the guffawing laugh is a sign of an emotional and impulsive character who finds it easy to make friends but just as easy to forget them. It also reveals lack of discipline and self-control, forgetfulness and a certain fickleness.

Explosive laugh

When a laugh bursts out unexpectedly and is irrepressible and joyous, it reveals an endearingly childlike and chiefly optimistic nature.

Sarcastic laugh

This belongs to people who have a critical mind, who are always on the alert and treat every aspect of life with irony and scepticism. They may have a disagreeable and sometimes pessimistic character. Often a sarcastic laugh conceals shyness and pride.

Feeble laugh

A feeble laugh indicates not only shyness but also very little vital energy. People who laugh like this are sometimes detached from reality.

Closed mouth laugh

This is typical of malicious people who set traps for others.

Mischievous laugh

An observant, curious mind belongs to this person, who seeks erotic sensations but is never vulgar.

Laugh interspersed with hiccups

This is a sign of a repressed nature and of someone who is unable to relieve tensions.

Artificial laugh

The artificial laugh is the stereotypical laugh which, through frequent professional use, becomes a habit in people who have to kowtow to clients or superiors. Otherwise it is the laugh of a snob and, in some cases, a forced laugh hides annoyance.

Laugh built around the 'a' vowel

If it is a long 'Ha, ha, ha, ha!' laugh it shows an open and communicative nature, a lively character, kindness and a fighting spirit.

Laugh built around the 'e' vowel

A 'He, he, he, he!' laugh is typical of people who are dissatisfied and enjoy seeing other people's weaknesses or foolishness. It is a derisory, and sometimes nasty, laugh, and easily misinterpreted as genuine.

Laugh built around the 'i' vowel

This is a laugh which indicates little emotional participation and lack of feeling. It may be found in people who are childishly malicious or repressed.

Laugh built around the 'o' vowel

A sign of a sophisticated and controlled nature, this laugh shows someone who tends to conceal their feelings for fear of other people's judgement. There is also an element of presumption and gentle scorn in this person, who sometimes likes to make fun of others.

Laugh built around the 'u' vowel

This laugh, with the lips pulled down, is typical of intellectuals or pseudo intellectuals, who love paradoxes and eccentricity. There is a certain affectation in their behaviour, which often masks neuroses and insecurity.

Teeth

All the details of the face and body are important and meaningful for physiognomy. The physiognomist becomes informed about the secrets of the psyche by studying physical details to which most people normally pay little attention. The structure and shape of the cheeks, teeth, tongue and temples are all significant. Many of these features, in particular the teeth and the tongue, are also revealing about a person's state of health.

A good doctor can often assess a patient's condition at a glance. Not many years ago it was common practice for skilful doctors to show that their intuitions were correct. Most lightning diagnoses can be based on a study of the details of a patient's face.

No one can compete with a doctor's diagnosis using physiognomy alone, but the implication is that careful observation of faces can contribute to medical diagnoses.

'It is the eyes and teeth that do more than anything else to create horror', says a top Hollywood make-up artist. And

85 per cent of Americans agree with him – for as one survey demonstrated, they believe that ugly, crooked teeth are a definite handicap in life. In another survey, children were shown pictures of faces with crowded teeth – which they all disliked. Pictures of protruding teeth had a similar effect on their young audience – revealing a deep psychological response.

Of course, higher standards of dentistry, hygiene, and cosmetic work have made everyone more aware of their teeth – and provided widely-available means to improve unappealing ones. Further evidence suggests that ugly teeth do not create problems in themselves, but someone who is very sensitive about their teeth may often try to hide them. They might conceal them during conversation, or repress natural smiles and laughter and become generally less sociable than those blessed with a dazzling set of pearly white teeth. On the whole, it is this withdrawn and unnatural behaviour which affects other people, not the teeth themselves.

Health is always an attractive quality in someone – suggesting positive characteristics such as vitality, optimism, energy and happiness. So strong teeth, whatever their shape, cannot help but create a good impression. We also associate them with youth, and, by association, with physical strength and beauty. Many people in the public eye have their teeth capped nowadays, in order to enhance their image. Meanwhile, in other parts of the world, teeth are deliberately blackened, filed, or knocked out altogether in ancient and painful ceremonies.

Neglected, badly-shaped, or unhealthy teeth can indicate a number of things. Some people care less than others about their appearance. This may show either a high-minded lack of vanity, an unworldly quality, or it may reveal someone whose attitude is 'Love me, love my faults'. This person might be rather arrogant and selfish. Beautifully cared-for teeth can also suggest self-consciousness, or a healthy regard for the body and a desire to be liked by everyone.

Reactions to teeth are therefore usually emotional – and not always accurate pointers to another person's true nature. Try to bear all these things in mind when practising the art of face reading, and avoid making negative judgements simply because you dislike what you see.

Tatum O'Neill displays perfect, regular teeth; signs of refinement and good dentistry

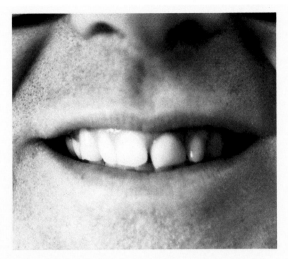

Wide, slightly crooked teeth with visible gaps denote energy and determination to succeed

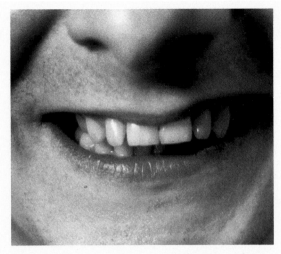

Small, even teeth point to a reserved, intelligent character

Wide teeth, close together
These teeth show good physical resistance and plenty of energy. They belong to people who appreciate the pleasures of good food and are likely to live to a ripe old age; they may have an aggressive side to their character.

Strong, pointed teeth
A lively, fighting spirit and someone who is sexually well balanced is indicated by these teeth.

Long teeth
Long teeth reveal an uncertain, diffident character. This person speaks and comes to decisions with caution.

Long teeth, wide apart
These reveal an indecisive, lazy nature. Some experts say that the gaps indicate financial luck.

Small, short teeth
This person has a penetrating mind but is sometimes reserved or inhibited. In some cases, these teeth are a sign of effeminacy.

Sharp, protruding teeth
When the incisors protrude, a combative, argumentative nature is to be found.

Teeth that are exposed at the top
This indicates an ability to observe life with detachment and self-control. It is also a sign of irony and coolness.

Yellow teeth
These are often a result of an organic disorder in childhood, but are no less likely to be strong and long-lasting than a set of dazzling white teeth. They can also mean excessive commitment to work, or this person may simply be a heavy smoker.

Dazzling teeth
These show a healthy person who has refined tastes.

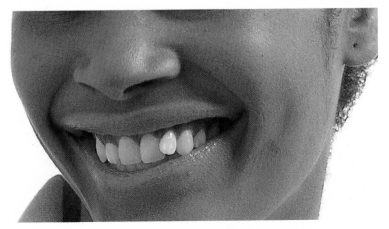

Long teeth mean a cautious, careful personality

Cheeks, tongue and temples

Cheeks

Full, fleshy cheeks
These indicate a sensual, exuberant nature. They are typical of people who attach importance to practical matters and who love to enjoy life.

Thin, hollow cheeks
A nervous, restless temperament is indicated by thin, hollow cheeks. These people seek inner harmony; in artists this is a sign of an agitated imagination and a yearning for perfection, sometimes combined with a hint of madness.

Wrinkled, thin, sagging cheeks
These are a sign of suffering, nutritional deficiencies or liver disorders. This person finds little to enjoy in life, and is likely to repress anger.

Round upper cheeks
If the cheeks are full and fleshy around the eyes, they indicate a generous, naive nature. Fond of practical jokes, these people are popular and have full social lives.

Cheeks with prominent cheek-bones
These are typical of people who are strong willed, dynamic and independent. They also reveal a person who on the one hand seeks ideals and love in life, but on the other hand is tenacious, ambitious and egocentric.

Flat cheeks
When the cheek-bones are not visible or not very pronounced, the cheeks denote a sober, controlled nature. This person may lack energy and have frequent changes of mood.

Dimpled cheeks
These indicate a naturally good-natured person, who has a sensual nature and tends to be fickle.

Red cheeks
If the cheeks are naturally red or blush easily, it is a sign of an emotional temperament, repressed passion, shyness and pride.

Pale cheeks
Sometimes these mean that the person is anaemic, but more often they belong to delicate, lazy people. If they are also cold, this means the subject lacks vitality.

Cheeks with a triangular hollow
This is an indication of animosity, an envious nature and inner suffering.

Curved cheeks
A thoughtful, communicative character is expressed by curved cheeks. This person's life will be made up of many meaningful and valuable experiences.

Tongue

Pointed tongue
This reveals a lack of sensuality, a tendency not to waste energy and to control spending.

Small, short tongue
The subject lives more in a world of fantasy than reality, attaching greater importance to his or her inner life than to material pleasures.

Very long, wide tongue
This person has strong instincts and a sensual nature. This tongue also reveals a person who may sometimes lie or be biased in his or her judgement in order to achieve personal goals.

Tongue which often licks the lips
This is a sign of an emotional, tense nature.

Tongue which runs over the teeth
This has an erotic appeal which is often unconscious. It denotes unfulfilled sexual desires.

Dry, rough tongue
This is a sign of dehydration and illness.

Tongue which bleeds and is hypersensitive
This is due to an inflammation of the oral cavity (stomatitis) or the use of drugs.

Temples

Dimpled temples
When the temples are concave they signal a delicate mind, intuition and also lack of vitality. If they are very much indented, there is a danger that this person will suffer physical weakness in later life.

Protruding temples
When the temples are full or actually protrude, they indicate a rational, lively, happy character.

Felicity Kendall has the prominent, curved cheeks of a good communicator. They also suggest ambition and a romantic spirit

The neck

The Marquis de Sade, from whose name the term 'sadism' is derived, had a short, fat neck, indicating sexual deviancy and ambition. The seventeen neck shapes which follow indicate other aspects of the personality.

Long, thin neck
This person has a keen, delicate sensibility and refined taste, coupled with acute intelligence. He or she tends to be easily influenced, to fall in love frequently and to be conditioned by his or her upbringing.

Long, sinuous neck
This shows an ability to get out of difficult situations and also shows adaptability. It belongs to someone with an unstable character, who is sometimes irrationally sympathetic or antipathetic towards others. He or she likes taking risks.

Thin, stiff neck
This person likes to be in command, is judgemental and sometimes intolerant. He or she has more nervous energy than physical energy, and tends to be mechanically, rather than instinctively, affectionate.

Thin neck with visible tendons
This denotes dissatisfaction and, sometimes, an envious nature. This person's health is delicate. He or she feels intense affection coupled with anxiety for loved ones.

Big, short neck
This bull's neck is a sign of remarkable physical resistance and sexual potency. Its owner is tenacious, ambitious and determined. He or she may have sudden bursts of temper or even sadistic tendencies.

Short, fat neck
This indicates frivolous, mischievous sensuality combined with greed for food and a certain indolence. It can indicate a glandular disorder.

Short, small neck
This denotes a lively and easily-influenced person, who is fundamentally good but outwardly fickle, touchy and argumentative.

Neck with a protruding throat
A very protruding neck at the throat often indicates an abnormal thyroid. It is consistently typical of excitable, neurotic and over-emotional people.

Neck craning forward
This is the so-called servant's neck. It indicates a servile, opportunist, curious and invasive character, but also one which is kind and always ready to offer help. *Savoir-faire* and diplomacy help the subject overcome difficulties.

Neck leaning to the right
This person is studious and has great powers of concentration. He or she is contemplative, sometimes dwells on the

past and becomes melancholy, but is generally given to high-minded thought.

Neck leaning to the left
These people have a rather superficial, prejudiced view of life. They tend to be frivolous and wasteful, acting on whim. They have good powers of intuition, are perceptive of others and choose suitable partners for themselves.

Neck leaning in various directions
When a person's neck is not straight, but bends in and out, it is a sign of uncertainty and falseness. He or she will often

Modigliani often painted women with elongated necks, suggesting grace, delicacy and refinement

change his or her opinion, depending on who he or she is talking to.

Straight, stiff neck
A very rigid neck denotes ambition and vanity. It belongs to people who assert themselves successfully.

Neck with protruding veins
A tendency towards anger and aggression, especially if the neck is quite short, is characteristic of this subject. He or she has a repressed nature and is liable to explode with anger unexpectedly.

Receding neck
This person is hesitant, fearful, cautious and defensive.

Long neck with protruding Adam's apple
Men with this neck have an analytical mind and are fastidious. They are cautious and ultra critical in their love lives, but, once they have given themselves over to love, they are sincere and faithful.

Round, well-proportioned neck
This belongs to a well-balanced and usually serene person who is kind to others.

The hair

The colour of head and facial hair, its thickness or baldness all convey a psychological message. Men who prefer to grow a beard or moustache to a certain length or style are making a statement about themselves. Exactly how the hair is worn depends on fashion as well as personal taste: a hair style is revealing about self-image only in the context of current trends. The beard and moustache once symbolized authority, yet the Romans insisted that their rulers should have smooth faces. European societies have always considered women's hair an important seductive tool.

Thin hair
Thin hair is a sign of a refined and affectionate nature. This person's health may be delicate.

Strong, thick hair
This belongs to realistic, practical people who also have an affinity with nature and strong primeval instincts. In male subjects it may also be a sign of violence.

Smooth, thin hair
This person is sensitive, loyal and gentle. He or she is organized and has a well-balanced personality.

Baby-fine blonde hair denotes sensitivity

Thin, wavy hair
A fine mind, vanity and an extrovert character combine in these people. They are romantic and tend to have wealthy friends and acquaintances.

Meanings linked to dark, curly hair only apply to European types

Fair hair
Generally fair hair indicates a delicate, idealistic, slightly phlegmatic temperament. Medically it is often linked to anaemia. If the hair is thin, it shows refinement; if it is coarse, vulgarity and materialism.

Red hair
Traditionally red hair signals a bad temper. In fact it is a sign of an extreme character, either very good or very bad in temperament.

Thick, wavy, red hair signals vitality and erratic emotions

Strong, wavy hair
This denotes a sanguine, impulsive, stubborn and courageous temperament. Beneath a tough veneer, the subject conceals great kindness.

Long hair
Women who grow their hair long are malleable, industrious and faithful. In men, long hair reveals a love of nature and a degree of exhibitionism.

Thin, fragile, split hair
When the hair is dull and thin, it is a sign of delicate health.

Black hair
Black hair belongs to sensual, jealous, energetic people who have a strong sense of justice and order. If the black hair is thin, they are also intellectual. If it is thick and coarse, they can also be rough.

Different colour hair and eyebrows
This shows an insincere character trying to create a dual personality.

A tendency to baldness
Baldness is usually due to the overproduction of male hormones. Psychologically, it reveals a tenacious, self-assertive character which suffers deep frustration in the face of failure.

Premature white hair
If a lot of white hair appears before old age, it signifies worry and pain; it is also a sign of a contemplative nature detached from reality.

Beards
Goatee beard
Men with goatee beards subconsciously want to be thought of as intellectuals or artists.

Bushy beard
Men who decide to grow thick beards may want to adorn the chin or mask a defect. Often they wish to emphasize their virility. Young men who want to appear older or more experienced will often grow a beard to gain prestige.

Long, flowing beard
Growing a long beard frequently reveals the aspiration for a deeper inner life; other men with long beards wish only to appear wiser or more thoughtful and introspective.

Beard and sideburns
A beard accompanied by sideburns can be a sign of originality, but it can also mean a romantic attachment to the past and to tradition.

Moustaches
Thin moustache
Men with thin moustaches often wish to appear strikingly refined and elegant. They are often clever and artistic, but may be extremely vain.

Bristly moustache
These men have an argumentative, sometimes aggressive nature, and find it hard to accept the judgement of others.

Thick moustache
This indicates an affectionate, proud nature and the wish to be noticed by the opposite sex. Many men grow thick moustaches out of an unconscious desire to follow their father's or grandfather's example.

Salvador Dali, surrealist painter and celebrated eccentric, displays his sinuous, slender moustache

Wrinkles

Every forehead has wrinkles, whether they are deep, thin, wavy or very faint. Wrinkles are either vertical or horizontal: vertical wrinkles are caused by intellectual work, thinking and by concentrating on spiritual problems. Horizontal wrinkles, on the other hand, belong to curious, observant people, who want to experience life to the full. They appear on the faces of humanitarian people who like to measure themselves constantly against reality.

Vertical wrinkles
These appear above the nose and reveal the intensity of the subject's intellectual strength. Doubts and inner worries lie behind a frowning forehead. Sometimes the same type of wrinkles indicate an irritable nature, so any assessment must be cautiously made to eliminate ambiguities. The expression in the eyes is therefore also important.

Vertical wrinkles and a tired, dull look
This is an indication of preoccupation and anxiety. However, beneath the façade lies a sensitive personality, sometimes frustrated but clever. The subject is probably just waiting for the opportunity to demonstrate his or her true worth and potential.

Vertical wrinkles, a tired look and frowning eyebrows
These belong to a diffident individual who tends to be calculating. This person is influential due to a charismatic personality. He or she is also a bit of a pessimist.

Vertical wrinkles, a lively look and eyes that never close
These belong to people who are continually searching for something, without knowing precisely what it is. They are often discontented and tend to blame others for their own disappointments. These subjects are forever occupied with artistic or intellectual pursuits which absorb every ounce of their energy. When they are tired, they can become hypochondriacal and typically suffer from nervous exhaustion.

Horizontal wrinkles
These belong to lively, outgoing people who are daily fascinated by life. They are observant, pragmatic and sympathetic towards others. These wrinkles can be found in young people who are eager to learn, have interesting experiences, and create opportunities for themselves.

Forehead with a few horizontal wrinkles
These people are naturally vivacious with eclectic ideas and a number of interests. Their gaze is almost always attentive and penetrating and their minds ready to grasp and to create stimuli. These are features of an original and mature personality.

Vertical wrinkles indicate powers of concentration

Horizontal wrinkles and frowning eyebrows
These belie a receptive, positively-orientated, intelligent and extremely curious person. He or she will have a strong character and generally never experience depression; he or she will tend to take charge of situations and will be hard-working and productive.

Horizontal wrinkles and a lively expression
The best quality of these people is mental versatility and the ability to reconsider and revise their opinions. Tolerance, a sense of justice and receptiveness to all that is new and unusual are coupled with an extraordinary amount of vitality and enthusiasm.

Horizontal wrinkles and a dull expression
This indicates almost the opposite of the preceding category. The subjects generally have closed minds and lack maturity of judgement. They also lack a certain amount of willpower, and tend to be absentminded, for they are lost in a world of their own.

Horizontal wrinkles on a fleshy forehead

These indicate a typically phlegmatic character. The subjects' surroundings affect them very little. They are generally thick-skinned and indifferent, and hence never learn from their mistakes.

Horizontal wrinkles on a bony forehead

These individuals need to take a more balanced, overall view of life. They pay too much attention to detail, overvaluing minor issues unjustifiably. They may have analytical powers, but they often lack the ability to reason.

Few wrinkles denote youth and a lively mind

A lively expression with few lines show a mercurial, optimistic personality

A bony forehead with horizontal lines often belongs to a perfectionist

Many fine lines can reveal a delicate constitution

High, narrow foreheads with many wrinkles indicate impractical intelligence

A fleshy brow wrinkles slowly, signalling a calm, unruffled nature

Eyebrows and eyelids

If you want to find out whether someone is passionate, capricious, calm or vivacious, much will be revealed by the eyelids and the curve of the eyebrows. The colour of the eyes and the pupils are also important factors in revealing a person's character.

Eyebrows
Normal
These denote a friendly, active nature with plenty of common sense. They also show an ability to organize and realize projects.
Bushy eyebrows
An obstinate, brave, argumentative nature and a fighting spirit drive the subject to follow ambitious goals.
Thin, almost non-existent eyebrows
Subjects with these eyebrows have insufficient willpower, an indecisive, sometimes weak, character, are sensitive and easily impressionable. A fear of making mistakes can make them passive and self-sacrificing.

Long, thick eyebrows
These are an indication of a lively, exuberant, tireless nature, of passion in love and total commitment for the most demanding of undertakings. Impulsiveness can lead these people to over-indulge occasionally.
Joined eyebrows
People with these eyebrows are easily disheartened and pessimistic. They tend to become lost in their thoughts or own inner world.
Short eyebrows
These belong to someone with a restless and capricious nature, who is subject to frequent mood changes. He or she has a critical, keen mind and can be too judgemental of others to make rapid friendships. In working life he or she has a strong sense of order.
Angular eyebrows
This dynamic, courageous person with eyebrows shaped like a circumflex also has an unpredictable and original temperament.

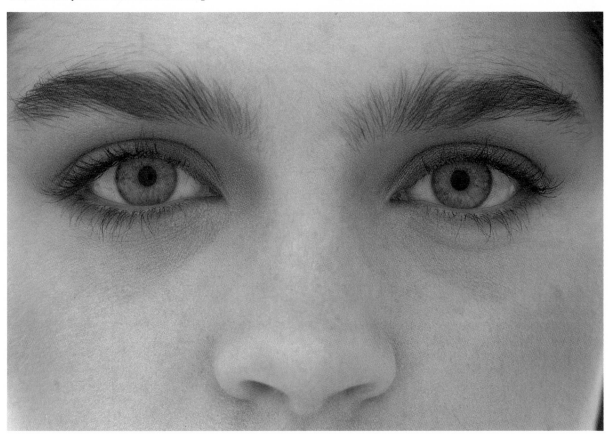

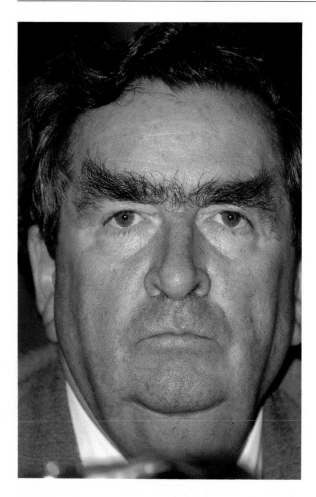

Politician Denis Healey's dramatic, bushy eyebrows reveal his ambitious nature

These eyebrows become thicker at the ends, signifying an inability to see things through. Variable energy levels can affect creative ability

Arched brows like these show an assertive, decisive thinker who likes to be in charge

Intelligent and manipulative, these eyebrows belong to people who work best in a team

Almost perfect eyebrows curve evenly, tapering to a fine point at the ends, and indicate a logical fair-minded individual

The reverse of the eyebrows top left, this pair reveals lack of ambition and foresight

Thick, bushy and uneven, these eyebrows indicate impulsiveness and a healthy constitution

Ruffled eyebrows

This person is insecure, but generous. Sometimes kind feelings are covered up by a surly manner, but nonetheless a warmer nature lies beneath the brusque façade.

Eyebrows very far apart

These eyebrows belong to altruistic, calm yet vivacious people. They have the ability to listen to and help others with great humanity whilst retaining their common sense.

Eyebrows slanting upwards

Though known as Mephistophelean eyebrows, these do not denote a devilish nature. They are typical of happy people who like to play practical jokes; often they modestly hide their own true feelings.

Low eyebrows

Low eyebrows on the whole indicate highly observant, balanced individuals; however, they can often be intransigent and egocentric as well.

René Descartes, French philosopher, displays the long, curved eyebrows of a passionate man

Eyelids
Large eyelids
These reveal a rational character and a good psychophysical balance. The subject puts the appropriate emphasis on every aspect of life.
Heavy eyelids
In many cases these indicate depression, inertia and apathy. If they are accompanied by an arrogant look, they indicate snobbery. Combined with a pensive look, they reinforce an already remarkable intellectual depth.
Eyelids which open and close frequently
These reveal nervousness, an emotional nature and an unconscious desire to protect the self from reality – as if the subject is prepared for something unpleasant to happen at any moment.
Raised lower lids
Raised lower lids are a sign of an affectionate, outgoing nature. These people love good food and drink and are playfully sensual.
Very low lower lids
When the white of the eye is visible below the pupil a nature which is prone to mysticism and contemplation is usually indicated.
Upper lid always raised
When the white of the eye is visible above the pupil the subject has a curious, inquiring mind, fears the unknown and is a daydreamer.

Eyeballs
White
White eyeballs are a sign of good health and a balanced character.
Bloodshot
Bloodshot eyes can denote a liver disorder. They can also be a sign of photophobia – irritation caused by sunlight or artificial light. Someone with a fever may have bloodshot eyes, or they may simply signal nervousness or a person with a short temper.
Yellow
Yellow eyeballs are often caused by hepatitis or an outflow of bile, in which case the person's character will become correspondingly intolerant and melancholy.

Marlene Dietrich plucked her eyebrows to achieve a slightly quizzical look. Their natural line would be much thicker and less stylish

The colour of the eyes

Eyes convey myriad messages and emotions. But eye colour can modify this silent language considerably. For example, it is well known that when your pupils expand and contract they are reacting to light. Yet they also dilate with pleasure and attraction, and grow smaller when you see something, or someone, you dislike. So light-coloured eyes are easier to read, while dark ones remain mysterious. Black eyes seem continually to be registering pleasure.

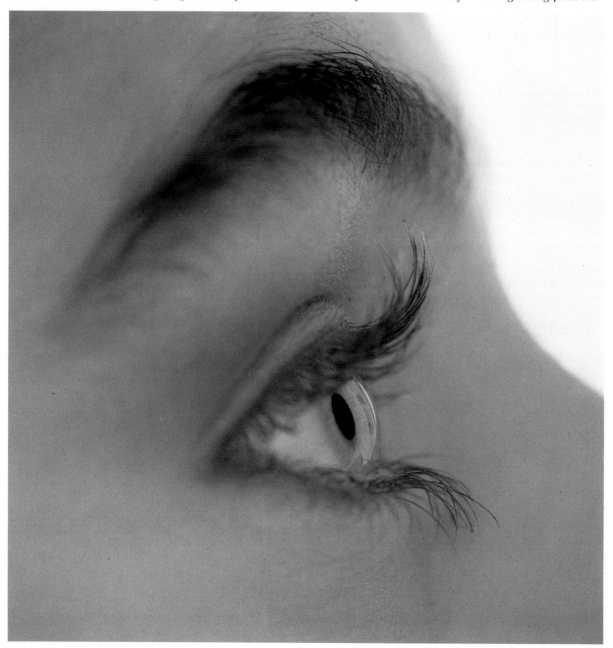

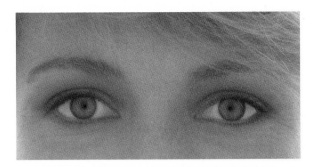

Wide-apart green eyes show intelligence and warmth

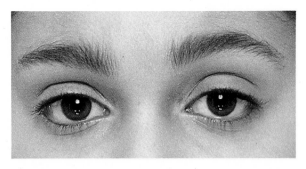

Stubborn, honest and moody is the message in these brown eyes

Black eyes
These reveal passion, sometimes hidden but irrepressible. This person's innate good taste and strong temperament help him or her to succeed.

Blue eyes
Strong intuition, dynamism and instinctiveness are characteristics of people with blue eyes. These subjects are sensitive, tactful people capable of giving their all to a great love or to a noble ideal. If the eye is china blue, a little dull and watery, it reveals a sluggish nature and a weak, but sensual, character.

Dark brown eyes
An obstinate, sometimes capricious, nature goes with brown eyes. These people have the ability to become deeply involved in routine activities. They react to the slightest injustice and are prone to sudden bursts of anger.

Hazel eyes
Someone with hazel eyes has a marked ability to organize and is also very practical. He or she is resistant to easy sentimentality and devoted to the search for an intelligent, sincere partner.

Grey eyes
Exceptional intelligence and the potential for achieving great things in the practical and commercial spheres belong to these subjects. They are not entirely lacking in fine feelings and innate good taste.

Green eyes
Kindness and generosity go with green eyes. A magnetic attraction for the opposite sex is often conveyed in the expression of these eyes. These subjects willingly make sacrifices out of love for their partner; but they also have a jealous and possessive nature. Sometimes they are excessively sensual, forgetting that in love too much emphasis on sensuality can be counterproductive.

Eyes very far apart
If there is more than a 3 cm distance between the inner corners of the eyes, it reveals aesthetic sense, a good memory and someone adept at solving problems.

Eyes very close
If the distance between the eyes is less than 2.5 cm, this person has an impressionable nature, is moody and prone to making harsh judgements of others.

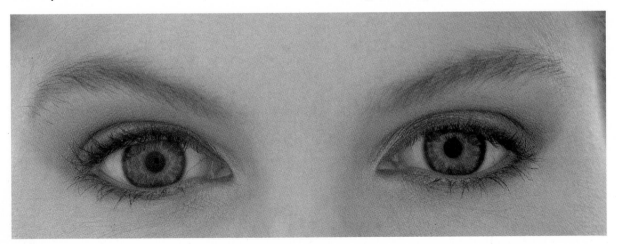

An intriguing mixture of colours reveals a complex personality

Hereditary features

Generations of a family belonging to different eras may have certain common features – that is, there may be a family resemblance. The Hapsburgs (pictured) ruled for centuries over the Austro-Hungarian empire. Their likeness is due to hereditary features which have been handed down from generation to generation.

In the Hapsburg faces this results in the principal family feature of the jutting chin, which they all have. Their mouths and eyes all have common characteristics, and so do the noses of Maximilian II, Philip V and, to an extent, Philip II. Any detailed examination will reveal a number of less obvious family resemblances which are not immediately apparent, such as the shape of the eyebrows and position of the hairline.

Scientists are only just beginning to unravel the mysteries of the genetic code. Messages encoded in our deoxyribonucleic acid (DNA) are responsible for both features and colouring; here three generations of Hapsburgs – Maximilian II, Philip II and Philip V – share the family chin. You can conduct your own research with the aid of family photographs: similar features often connect with certain characteristics or talents. Dynasties like Britain's Royal Family often display features which can be traced back centuries

PHILIPPVS V.

PHILIPPVS V. Ludovici Delphini Franciæ ex Mariâ Annâ Victoriâ
Bauariæ Ducibus secundogenitus, ac Nepos LVDOVICI MAGNI Galliaru Regis
et MARIÆ THERESÆ Caroli II. Hispaniarum Regis defuncti sororis, pridem
nuncupatus Dux Andegauensis, ad Hispaniæ Monarchiæ successione uocatus
Parisijs primu ab Auo Ludouico Rex salutatus die 16. Nouemb. 1700, egre-
giæ indolis, prudentiæ, ac pietatis specimina illustria statim edidit,
quibus Hispaniæ ueterem splendorem se restiturum, Christiano que
Orbi maiora, semper prosperitatum incrementa se tributuru spondet
DEVS. O. M. tantu Regem diu seruet incolumem et ad Hispaniæ feli-
citate Catholicoru Principum concordiam Italiæ nostra incolumitatem,
et Religionis profectu natum, se, suis que maioribus digna prole, et
nunquam desiturâ posteritate fortunet. Natus Parisijs die 19.
xbris 1683.

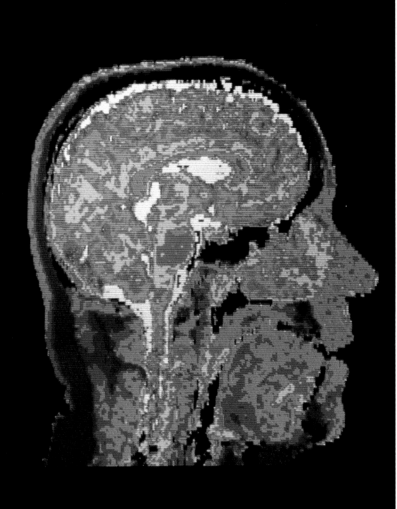

5

Phrenology and the Brain

Phrenology, the study of the shape, proportions and bumps on the skull, is a separate art to that of physiognomy. However, many physiognomists suggest that a combination of both can give more accurate results than either one alone.

Experts have categorized forty bumps on the human head of varying shapes and sizes, which reveal tendencies and peculiarities in each individual. If you can successfully identify these bumps, you will be able to make an accurate interpretation of their meaning. It can be useful to discover hidden talents, especially if you or your friends are considering a change of career. Parents, too, could use phrenology to see what kind of abilities their children possess. This was common practice until the nineteen-twenties; after the twenties it seems to have died out almost completely. Skull-reading was first practised in the eighteenth century by Dr Franz Joseph Gall, but his work was not taken seriously by other doctors. It was not until one of his followers, George Combe, gained the support of doctors and scientists in Britain that phrenology came to be studied much more widely.

Phrenology scholars believe that many of the talents of each individual (which correspond to particular parts of the brain) are indicated by these bumps. The expression, for example, that a person has a head for maths, usually refers to a generic gift that person has. The expression becomes literal, and not just metaphorical, through a phrenological examination of the bumps on their head.

Some bumps are barely perceptible and may be small and round or horn-shaped. Others are more obvious. To check your own, simply feel your head while looking in the mirror.

Phrenology

Phrenology, or the art of reading the skull, dates back to the eighteenth century. It was invented by Dr Franz Joseph Gall, a physician working in Vienna. He began developing his theories at school, where he became increasingly intrigued by what he saw as the close connection between appearance and ability. Why, for example, did boys with rather prominent eyes seem to have the best memories? Could physical characteristics reveal talents or abilities?

Gall's research was very thorough and sometimes rather macabre, for not only did he examine the living, he also scrutinized the heads of criminals after execution. The famous and gifted, infamous, imprisoned and patients in mental asylums were all subjected to Gall's painstaking observations.

Eventually, Gall concluded that regions of the brain corresponded to various personality traits and abilities. When someone is born with, for example, a gift for languages, the relevant part of their brain is more developed. This development, Gall claimed, was mirrored in the shape of the skull, where bumps and indentations identified mental and emotional leanings. Although his work inspired the general public, Gall was ridiculed by other doctors and condemned by the Church authorities. He died in Paris in 1828, a poor and embittered man.

One of Gall's British followers, George Combe, had greater success, and found support amongst scientists and doctors. Combe's phrenological readings of prisoners' heads were very impressive, for he was able to come up with facts which matched prison records he had never seen. Although he, too, was a controversial figure, his book was a best-seller – and as a result phrenology continues to be studied today.

Successful head-hunting

Like palmistry, successful phrenological readings depend upon a mixture of knowledge and intuition. The basic bumps are rather like letters of an alphabet – once you have mastered them all you can begin to make sentences. Do not forget that people are often contradictory. Someone might be mean when it comes to paying household bills, for instance, but very generous with gifts.

Never base any judgement on just one area – and do not forget that each quality has a range of interpretation. Is someone ambitious, with clearly thought-out goals and a healthy desire to succeed? Or are they a power-mad, selfish person who will stop at nothing to achieve their ends? Facial indications are also important, for they can confirm or modify traits suggested by the head.

George Combe's penetrating gaze uncovered the secrets of the skull

Dr. Franz Joseph Gall, physician and founder of phrenology

1 The music bump
A bump here is a sign of natural musical ability and of general creativity in the artistic field.

2 The money bump
A protrusion here reveals the urge to earn and the ability to accumulate money.

3 The mathematics bump
This appears in the centre of the temple. It is a sign of a scientific, rational mind, sometimes indicating a preference for infinitesimal algebraic calculations.

4 Greed bump
This is found in people who do not know how to control their intake of food, which to them is one of life's greatest pleasures.

5 Business bump
This protruberance above the ear is a sign of practicality, business acumen, a realistic, and sometimes sceptical, mind. These people find it hard to relax.

6 Courage bump
Found behind the ear, the courage bump is a sign of an audacious character which seeks adventure and defends the weak. If it is too pronounced, this bump can reveal violence and aggression.

7 Strength bump
This corresponds to vital energy, both physical and mental.

8 Love bump
This can be seen if the side of the neck is prominent. It is a sign of sensuality, passion, jealousy and sexual energy.

9 Fighting bump
This denotes a person with a combative nature who is competitive and likes to put their strength to the test. It shows remarkable physical resistance.

10 Bump of affection
Even a light bump here is a sign of an affectionate nature. It indicates a special ability to love with dedication, fidelity, tenderness and without reservation.

11 Motherhood or fatherhood bump
If this area is well developed, it indicates a strong maternal or paternal instinct and tenderness towards children.

12 Aesthetic bump
A bump between the nose and the forehead is typical of people who have pronounced aesthetic taste, natural elegance and a love of beauty.

13 Studious bump
A protuberance in the centre of the forehead is typical of people who have a thirst for knowledge and a good memory. It also denotes a particular interest in history, archaeology and tradition.

14 Bump of widening knowledge
This belongs to a meditative mind which likes to analyse and think deeply about everything.

15 Justice bump
This is very developed in people who have a strong sense of justice and who are able to weigh up the pros and cons and rights and wrongs of every situation fairly.

16 Kindness bump
A bump on the line of ascent, going up the head, is a sign of a generous, kind and good nature. In women it reveals depth of feeling, in men, a protective nature.

17 Bump of spirituality
A small mound at the top of the head is a sign of heightened spiritual and moral qualities, whether in the religious, political or social spheres.

18 Bump of willpower
If this area is raised, it reveals willpower, tenacity and reliability in a person.

19 Bump of domination
This protruberance reveals decisive, authoritarian and despotic tendencies.

20 Bump of concentration
This is linked to that part of the brain which determines concentration and intellectual energy. It shows an aptitude for literary and philosophical pursuits.

21 Family bump
This area is developed in subjects who are very attached to their families.

22 Travel bump
A bump here is a sign of a dynamic nature and of someone who is adventurous, loves to travel, explore and move from one place to another. He or she will readily adapt to unusual or exotic cultures.

23 Bump of reason
This is typical of logical, rational people who have very lively minds.

24 Bump of mental flexibility
This is a sign of broadmindedness and an open, flexible and receptive mind.

25 Bump of conformity
This bump is often found in people who are fashion-conscious and imitate media stars, but are otherwise conventional and conform to the norm.

26 Bump of idealism
This bump is particularly obvious in people who determinedly adhere to ideals. It also reveals a strong sense of duty and wealth of spirit.

27 Bump of optimism
This person tends to have an optimistic view of life and has faith in others.

28 Bump of success
This is the bump of someone who channels all their energy into life.

29 Critical bump
This shows the ability to criticize others and oneself. This person has excellent powers of observation.

30 Objectivity bump
The objectivity bump belongs to people who have the gift of being able to put themselves in someone else's place and understand their point of view.

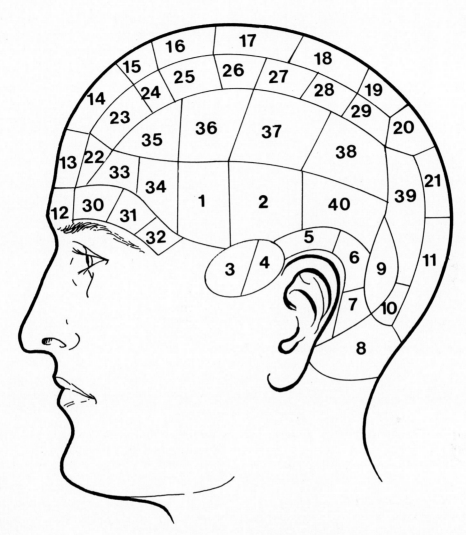

31 Colour bump
This reveals someone with strong colour sense, whether it is manifested in painting or in dress, in photography or in choice of furniture

32 Bump of meticulousness
A bump here is to be found in people who love precision, order and discipline.

33 Organization bump
This is very pronounced in people who are able to manage their time efficiently. They are great achievers who fill every minute from dawn till dusk.

34 Rhythm bump
Many drummers, percussion players and singers have this bump, which is a sign of a strong sense of rhythm.

35 Gregariousness bump
This bump is often found in people who are lively, communicative and able to spread happiness to everyone they meet.

36 Originality bump
This indicates an original character and a refined mind. These people can be eccentric or avante-garde.

37 Bump of inventiveness
A bump here expresses pronounced creative talents.

38 Bump of fame
This is found in many famous people. It indicates the desire to be known and acclaimed in the public eye.

39 Bump of caution
This cautious person chooses friends carefully and exercises rigorous self-control.

40 'Savoir-faire' bump
This reveals a diplomatic, courteous and tactful person with an astute mind.

The brain

The ability for mathematics or literature, logic or fantasy depends on which half of the brain is best developed, the left or the right. These two cerebral hemispheres are linked to a cluster of nerve fibres, the *corpus callosus*, which decodes information from the sense organs and is the seat of intelligence, thought and memory. Each of the two hemispheres has separate functions. The left side, where the motor nerves cross over, controls the right side of the body and the right side controls the left side of the body. The left hemisphere governs the faculty for logic, reasoning, mathematical calculation, verbal expression and sense of time; the right hemisphere governs artistic and musical ability, creativity, the imagination, intuitive thought and spatial awareness.

The powers of the brain are vast, and human beings use only an infinite fraction of its resources. It is a miraculous instrument made up of 16 billion cells which can process about 200 billion messages per second. Contrary to an erroneous common belief, it is not the weight of the brain which determines a person's intelligence. The brain of the great physicist, Albert Einstein, weighed 1,375 g, while the brains of far less intelligent people weigh more. What counts, however, is the quality of your grey matter. One of the two hemispheres will have a stronger controlling force – which one will come to the fore in early childhood, and will eventually determine your vocation in life.

The left hemisphere
When the left hemisphere is functioning fully, it controls the right side of the body and therefore makes it easier to use the right hand to write with, as this hand will have greater strength. As the left side also controls speech, if this side is well developed then, with practice, its owner can become a brilliant conversationalist, lecturer, lawyer or sales representative. Scientific and economics studies, social and political research, cybernetics and astronomy may all be improved through the development of this side of the brain. It controls the notion of time as well, so it is important for studying history and archeology, and for acquiring a knowledge of antiques.

An injury to the left side of the brain can cause grave speech and communication difficulties; it can affect the sense of time (the subject may forget what day it is), and can cause the subject to become left-handed, by weakening the abilities of the right hand side of the body.

The right hemisphere
A well-developed right hemisphere results in a preference for painting, music, psychology, psychoanalysis, religion and literature. It can result in someone becoming an original and brilliant writer, inventor, film director, photographer or occultist. The right hemisphere activates the brain's electrical impulses, and can awaken the kind of powers that belong to mediums, hypnotists, telepathically and psychokinetically gifted people. It governs the ability to look beyond material matter, and will be well developed in faith healers and in those who are able to interpret the significance of dreams.

A famous Neapolitan medium called Eusapia Paladino, who normally used her right hand, suddenly became left-handed each time she went into a trance during seances. Her mind instinctively connected with the psychic powers of the right hemisphere when she went into a trance. As the right hemisphere controls the left side of the body, it caused her to become left handed.

A major or minor injury to the right hemisphere impairs the subject's sense of balance and whereabouts, and can cause serious disorientation; he or she may forget streets, places and locations. Motor activity will be reduced, making every manual movement, from lighting a cigarette to lacing up shoes or knotting a tie, very difficult. Imaginative ability will be impaired, rendering fairy tales, the unreal and science-fiction incomprehensible. In some cases, when the right hemisphere is gravely damaged, the subject stops dreaming at night and the psyche is deprived of the freedom of escape through dreams.

The ideal would be to use both right and left cerebral hemispheres to the maximum. There are people who, having trained their minds using special techniques, have succeeded in performing two tasks at once, answering practical questions on the telephone, for example, (which sets the left hemisphere in motion) while continuing to paint, play the piano or read a novel (all of which depend on the right hemisphere).

There is a simple exercise you can do which brings out this bilateral ability. Put on a blindfold and try to guess what an object is (even one that is hard to identify) which is placed in your left hand. The right side of the brain will help distinguish the characteristics of the mystery object while, at the same time, the left side of the brain will supply you with the correct words to describe it perfectly.

Developing the right hemisphere is important if you want to become a talented physiognomist. Both sound knowledge and intuition are required in every kind of character analysis – think of the inspired hunches that, against all logic or reason, lead detectives to a solution. With the help of this book you, too, could become an investigator. But your investigations will be uncovering something even more fascinating – the mysterious complexities of human nature.

Index

Acknowledgments

Editor: Carolyn Pyrah
Consultant Physiognomist: Jane Lyle
Translation: Lesley Bernstein Studios
Art Editor: Sandra Horth
Design: Carole Perks
Artwork: Jim Robins
Picture Research: Julia Pashley
Production Controller: Garry Lewis

The publishers would like to thank the following organizations for providing the photographs on the following pages:
BBC Hulton Picture Library 85 right; Camera Press Ltd 48, 65; ET Archive 85 left; Mary Evans Picture Library 22 left, 84, 88, 89; Gamma/FSP 12, 20, 23, 51, 62, 76, 80; Ronald Grant Archive 6, 81; John Hillelson Agency/M. Huteau 60; The Kobal Collection 26, 58; London Features International 71; Octopus Publishing Group/Chris Dawes 29, 69 below; Sandra Lousada 15 right, 16 right, 17 above, 21 below, 32, 35 above and below, 36, 38 left, 43 left, 53, 54, 56, 57, 64 above and below, 74, 75 above and below left, 75 right, 79, 82, 83 above left, above right and below; Eamonn J. McCabe 17 below, 18, 19 above and below, 66; Stuart MacLeod 42, 44 left and right; Duncan McNicol 46 above right; Tim Simmons 52; Victor Yuan 59; Science Photo Library 86.